PC TROUBLESHOOTING

in easy steps

STUART YARNOLD

**COMPUTER
STEP**

In easy steps is an imprint of Computer Step
Southfield Road . Southam
Warwickshire CV47 0FB . England

http://www.ineasysteps.com

Notice of Liability

Every effort has been made to ensure that this book contains accurate and current information. However, Computer Step and the author shall not be liable for any loss or damage suffered by readers as a result of any information contained herein.

Trademarks

Microsoft® and Windows® are registered trademarks of Microsoft Corporation. All other trademarks are acknowledged as belonging to their respective companies.

Printed and bound in the United Kingdom

ISBN 1-84078-132-7

Table of Contents

1 | **Troubleshooting Techniques** | **7**
Introduction | 8
Strategy | 10
Undo Recent Changes | 11
Read the Instructions | 13
Elimination & Substitution | 14

2 | **Bootup Troubleshooter** | **15**
Power Supplies | 16
Monitor | 17
Beep Codes | 18
Motherboard | 19
Graphics Card | 20
PC Fails to Complete Bootup | 21
Boot Procedure | 22
Manufacturers' Beep Codes | 23

3 | **Startup Troubleshooter** | **25**
Windows Refuses to Start | 26
Safe Mode | 27
Windows Won't Start in Safe Mode | 28
Windows Setup | 31
Windows Starts in Safe Mode | 32
Startup Programs | 34
Resource Conflicts | 35
Re-install Windows | 36

4 | **Shutdown Troubleshooter** | **37**
Fast Shutdown (Win 98 Only) | 38
Exit Sound File | 39
Temporary Folders | 40
Windows Initialisation Files | 41
Startup Programs | 43
Advanced Power Management | 44

5 | **Windows Setup Troubleshooter** | **45**
Preparation | 46
Setup Fails | 47
Clean Installation | 48
Setup Error Messages | 49

Hard Drive Troubleshooter 51

6

Hard Drive Failure	52
Hard Drive Is Not Being Recognised	53
Hard Drive Is Being Recognised	54
Performance Issues	55
New Drive Won't Boot	59
Common Hard Drive Error Messages	60

DVD/CD/Floppy Drive Troubleshooter 61

7

Drive Doesn't Work	62
CD Problems	64
DVD Problems	65
DVDs/CDs Don't Auto Play	66
Floppy Disk Problems	67

Memory Troubleshooter 69

8

Diagnosis	70
Too Many Applications Running	71
Virtual Memory	72
Hard Disk Space	73
Retained Memory	74

Display/Graphics Troubleshooter 75

9

Flickering Display	76
Incorrect Display	77
Can't Change Resolution/Colour Depth	78
Miscellaneous Image Faults	80

Sound Troubleshooter 81

10

No Sound	82
Sound Card	84
General Sound Problems	85
CD-ROM Drive has no Sound	88

Resource Conflict Troubleshooter 89

11

What is a Resource Conflict?	90
Device Manager	91
Identifying Resource Conflicts	92
Resolving Resource Conflicts	93
Device Manager Error Codes	97

System Instability Troubleshooter — 99

12

Strategy — 100
Dealing with a Frozen or Hung PC — 101
Causes of System Instability — 102
Common Instability Error Messages — 106

Printing Troubleshooter — 109

13

Printer Doesn't Print — 110
Files Print Slowly — 112
Poor Print Quality — 113
Software Settings — 114

Scanner Troubleshooter — 115

14

Scanner Doesn't Work — 116
Performance Issues — 117

Modem Troubleshooter — 121

15

Modem Doesn't Dial — 122
Modem Diagnostics Test — 123
Software Configuration — 124
Modem Driver — 126
Modem Passes Diagnostics Test — 127

Keyboard Troubleshooter — 129

16

Keyboard Failure — 130
Cleaning Your Keyboard — 131
Keyboard Printing Strange Characters — 132
Caps Lock — 134

Mouse Troubleshooter — 135

17

Mouse is Dead — 136
Mouse Movement is Jerky — 137
Turbo Charge Your Mouse — 138
Mouse Keys — 140

Network Troubleshooter   141

18

Isolating the Problem   142
One or More PCs Malfunctioning   143
Network Adapters   144
Network Client   145
Network Protocols   146
Computer Names   148
File and Print Sharing   149
Troubleshooting Network Hardware   150
Unable to Share Resources   152
Pinging   153

Internet Troubleshooter   155

19

Unable to Connect to the Internet   156
Intermittent Connections   158
Slow Connections   160
Unable to Access Particular Sites   162
Common Error Messages   163

Email Troubleshooter   165

20

Internet Connection   166
ISP Software Setup   167
Email Software Setup   169
Message Rules   171
Problems Sending Email   172

Troubleshooting Utilities   173

21

ScanDisk   174
Disk Cleanup   175
Disk Defragmenter   176
System Restore (Windows ME)   177
Maintenance Wizard   178
System Information   179
Dr Watson   180
System Configuration Utility   181
System File Checker (Windows 98)   182
Startup Disk   183
How to use a Startup Disk   184
Third Party Utilities   185

Index   187

Troubleshooting Techniques

Troubleshooting computers is not easy. It can be like looking for a needle in a haystack at times. However, there are things you can do which will help to swing the odds in your favour to a certain extent.

This chapter discusses the type of things that you ought to be considering before you get knee deep in silicon chips and circuit boards.

Covers

Introduction | 8

Strategy | 10

Undo Recent Changes | 11

Read the Instructions | 13

Elimination & Substitution | 14

Chapter One

Introduction

This book has been written with the aim of helping those unfortunate enough to be faced with a malfunctioning computer, to hopefully, not only understand *why* it's malfunctioning, but more importantly, how to get the thing going again.

Obviously, it's impossible to cover every conceivable fault, so instead we concentrate on the more serious ones, such as failure to boot up and other problems that are more likely to occur.

Clearly the most serious problem that anyone is likely to encounter is a PC which simply refuses to start. There are literally a hundred and one reasons why this can happen, a fact which makes it one of the most difficult computer faults to diagnose and repair. For this reason the first two chapters in this book are devoted entirely to this issue and provide a comprehensive step by step guide to bringing your PC back to life.

Crashes and lockups, while less serious, are a common and irritating part of a PC user's life. See the **System Instability Troubleshooter** for the low- down on this type of problem and what to do about it.

Incomprehensible error messages such as *General Protection Fault* and *This program has performed an Illegal Operation* are another frequent annoyance. Find out what they mean and how to stop them showing their faces again.

Millions of people are now using the Internet and every single one of them, at one time or another, will have problems – logging on, broken connections, sending & receiving email etc. The **Modem, Internet** and **Email Troubleshooters** cover this subject in detail with easy to follow faultfinding procedures.

Each chapter of the book examines a different part of the system, detailing likely faults and a systematic procedure for isolating and repairing them. All relevant terminology is explained to make the various procedures as clear as possible.

Please note that the book makes no attempt to troubleshoot specific problems with an item of hardware but rather to just identify a particular hardware device as faulty, if that is indeed the case. Having done so, it's up to the reader to either get the device repaired or replaced.

This raises a pertinent question – is it worth getting hardware repaired?

In the unlikely event of you being unfortunate enough to have a hardware device fail on you, weigh up the pros and cons before spending money on having it repaired. It might not make economic sense.

Taking a faulty motherboard as an example, while it's obviously possible to get it repaired, in practical terms it wouldn't make much sense, as it would in all probability cost as much if not more than buying a new one. Furthermore, unless it was brand new to start with, you would be spending good money to repair something that's probably obsolete or soon to be so. Computer technology advances at a frightening rate. Bear this in mind.

You will find that when troubleshooting a computer you are dealing predominantly with software. As Windows is the main software application on your PC, this means that in effect you are either troubleshooting Windows itself or troubleshooting *with* Windows (for example, you may be using the Windows utility *ScanDisk* to check your hard disk).

Throughout we have endeavoured to keep things as concise and relevant as possible. We have also tried to avoid the failing found in many troubleshooting books of telling a reader what to do but not explaining *how* to do it.

Finally, remember that the key to successful troubleshooting whether it be your computer or your car engine, lies in a considered and logical approach. Establish all the possibilities and then eliminate them one by one.

Good luck.

Strategy

If you decide to attempt your own repairs, try to resist the temptation to dive in head first.

Thinking before you act can save a lot of potential time and head scratching.

When faced with that most familiar of computer problems, a hung or frozen PC, hit Ctrl+Alt+Delete, before doing anything else. This brings up the Close Program box which shows you all the programs running and which one is causing the problem. Try and close the offending program from here.

Take any group of people, individually present them with the same problem in the same set of circumstances and you can be sure that the ways they go about tackling it will vary widely. One person will go at it like a bull in a china shop while another will do just the opposite, carefully examining the problem from all angles before doing anything.

Assuming this problem is a computer that refuses to work properly, which reaction is the best in terms of finding the solution? Well, who's to say? A lot depends on the circumstances. For example one person might need his PC back in a hurry and therefore take the bull in a china shop approach hoping for a quick fix while someone else might have all the time in the world and will thus carefully weigh up all the options before making a move. Jim Bullinachinashop might get lucky and stumble across the answer in five minutes flat while John Carefullyweighupalltheoptions might take several hours before finally working out what the problem is.

However, if you were to ask who is the more *likely* to solve the problem then the answer has to be John Carefullyweighupalltheoptions every time. An impatient and ill-considered approach is definitely not the most practical way to go about repairing computers.

Whichever approach you do decide to take, even a few minutes initial thought about what's happening (or not happening as the case may be) before actually doing anything, can save a lot of subsequent time and trouble. Often there are obvious steps to take before trying something more drastic. A good example of this is the familiar lockup or freeze. So many people immediately reach for the reset button and thus risk corrupting their hard drive, rather than hitting *Ctrl+Alt+Del* and attempting to isolate and close down the program causing the lockup. This can cause further problems.

Talk to any computer repair shop and they'll tell you that most computer faults are user induced and are a result of those users not doing things as they should. Bear this in mind.

Undo Recent Changes

One of the first things to consider is what were you doing on the PC immediately prior to the fault manifesting itself. If you can identify something specific then very often simply 'undoing' it will eliminate the problem.

For example you may have been doing any of the following:

- Downloading from the Internet

- Installing a peripheral, i.e. a new scanner.

- Upgrading your PC with a new card, i.e. a graphics card

- Deleting a program

- Installing a program

- Running a program

- Changing your PC's settings

- Shutting down your PC the wrong way

- Maintenance

There are hundreds of thousands of known viruses, the vast majority of which are spread via the Internet and their effects can mimic literally any computer fault. So if your PC starts giving trouble after downloading from the Internet there is a very good chance that it has picked up a virus. If you suspect this to be the case then you must obtain an up-to-date virus program and check your system with it.

Installing new hardware is a common cause of problems and is usually due to the new hardware device taking the resources allocated to an existing hardware device. This problem can usually be sorted out via *Control Panel, System, Device Manager*. See the **Resource Conflict Troubleshooter** for more details.

If like most people you enjoy tinkering with your PC's settings, try and restrict your 'fiddling' to the cosmetic side of things where you can't do any harm. Otherwise be sure to make a note of any changes you make.

Often we install a program to try out and then having decided we don't want it, delete it. With most programs there is no problem. However there are some which simply refuse to go quietly. The usual problem is that these programs use or 'borrow' files and then when they are deleted, take these files with them. Any other programs on the PC which need these files will then not run correctly, if at all. The cure for this is to re-install the affected program.

There are occasions when simply running a particular program will cause problems. It will either have become corrupted or is incompatible with something else on the system. The result will usually be lockups and crashes. Deleting and then re-installing it will usually cure the fault.

Windows is a very customisable operating system and allows the user to make all manner of changes to its default settings. This also applies to much of the systems hardware. However there are parts of the system where changes can have adverse effects on the PC's performance. Examples are the *BIOS* and the *registry*. The best policy when experimenting with settings, is to make a written note of any changes made. If there are any subsequent problems then you'll be able to reverse them.

Many problems are caused by not exiting Windows correctly and can be corrected by rebooting and doing it the right way. Only use your reset button when your PC is frozen solid.

There is most definitely a right way and a wrong way to shut down or restart your computer. The right way is to select *Start > Restart* or *Start > Shutdown*. You can also do a soft reboot by hitting *Ctrl + Alt + Delete*. The wrong way is to hit the reset button or power off button. This can corrupt any program that might be running, or worse, the hard drive itself. Usually though, the effects are minor and can be repaired by exiting in the proper manner and then running a disk utility such as *ScanDisk*.

If, for any reason you have been delving inside the system case, it's quite possible that you have inadvertently loosened or even disconnected something, a cable or expansion card for example. Try and retrace your steps, checking everything in the area in which you were working, making sure all boards and cables are firmly seated in their sockets.

Read the Instructions

Some applications and hardware can have incompatibility problems with other devices on your PC. If this is the case you'll need to find out what these are and how to sort them out. If you look on the installation disk you'll usually find a file called 'Setup Instructions' or 'Read Me'. If you are having problems always have a look at these. It can save you a lot of time.

Another frequent cause of problems, particularly when installing a new hardware device, is failure to read the installation instructions. Some devices are very simple to install while others require a bit more attention. For example, it's not uncommon for some devices or programs to be sold with known bugs leading to incompatibility with other hardware/software. There will usually be a file named 'README' on the installation disk detailing issues of this type and ways round them. Taking a few minutes to read the instructions can save hours of head scratching and frustration.

All you have to do is right-click on the appropriate disk drive in *My Computer* and then click *Open*. This will reveal the contents of the disk.

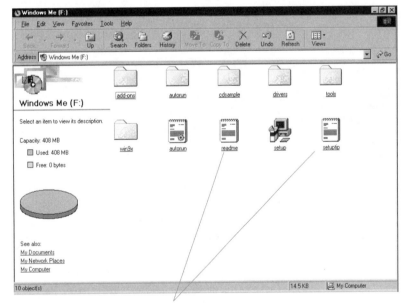

This screenshot taken from the Windows ME CD shows a *readme* and *setuptip* file. How many people have ever read them though?

Elimination & Substitution

Elimination

Sometimes you'll have a fault with a myriad of possible causes. It will be a head scratcher knowing where to even start. It's in situations like this that you'll need to adopt the 'John Carefullyweighupalltheoptions' approach.

What you've got to do is think logically and eliminate as many possibilities as you can in the order of likelihood. Start by undoing any recent changes made to the system. Then remove or disable as much of the systems hardware as possible. Disconnect any peripherals such as printers and scanners. Uninstall any suspect software. In this way you can eliminate many of the possibilities and gradually the picture will become clearer. Reboot after every change you make. If for example, you disconnect all your peripherals in one go and then reboot successfully, you won't know which peripheral was causing the problem.

Substitution

If and when you carry out an upgrade to your system, make a point of keeping the old component in a safe place. If you should subsequently have problems with the new component, you can use the old one to check it with.

The easiest and best way to check a component in your system is to substitute it with one you know to be good. It's also the only way to be absolutely certain that a particular component is either good or bad. A typical example would be when your monitor is dead on bootup. The most likely causes of this are the monitor itself or the graphics card. But which one? It shouldn't be too difficult to beg, steal or borrow a monitor from a friend or neighbour or connect yours to their system. This method can save untold hours of troubleshooting but does rely on a supply of spare components which will probably not be readily available. However, many people do upgrade their computers and keep the original parts for just this sort of purpose. A few phone calls to your acquaintances could well unearth what you are looking for.

Bootup Troubleshooter

Is there a computer owner anywhere in the world who hasn't at some stage switched on his machine only to find that the damned thing simply refuses to respond, either staring blankly back at him or presenting him with some cryptic message or other. Very few in all probability, but if you are one of the lucky ones, be assured your luck will eventually run out.

When it does, you may well find that resolving the problem is a far from simple task. If you follow the troubleshooting procedures in this chapter, however, you should be able to get your machine up and running without having to resort to help lines and the like.

Covers

Power Supplies | 16

Monitor | 17

Beep Codes | 18

Motherboard | 19

Graphics Card | 20

PC Fails to Complete Bootup | 21

Boot Procedure | 22

Manufacturers' Beep Codes | 23

Chapter Two

Power Supplies

Absolutely the first thing to check when your PC appears to be 'dead', is the power supply. Don't forget to check the external (mains) power supply as well.

So, you've switched on and discovered that all is not well. You will have one of two basic problems:

- The PC appears to be dead, i.e. the monitor is blank

- The PC won't boot up, i.e. it starts but then stops before completion

Let's start with the first scenario – a PC with no obvious signs of life.

The first thing to establish is whether you have power available to your PC. This principle applies to any item of electronic or electrical equipment, not just computers, and in this case is easily established by observation.

The easiest way to establish that your power supply unit is operational, is to check that the fan is working and that the keyboard lights are on.

Are the LEDs (lights) on the system case lit and is the power supply fan blowing? Do you see any lights on your keyboard? If the answer to any of these questions is yes, then the systems power supply is operational.

If the answer is no, then check the following:

- Is there power at the wall socket? Plug another appliance into it, if that works then the socket is OK.

- Are you using a surge suppressor or some similar device? If so, try removing or bypassing it and see if that cures the problem.

Computer power cables are usually the same type used with electric kettles and some other household appliances. This makes it a simple task to check them by substitution.

- Next, check the PC's power cable. Try substituting it with your electric kettle cable, these are usually the same type.

- Most PCs also have an on/off switch at the rear of the case. Check that this isn't in the off position.

If none of these is causing the problem then the PC's power supply unit is defective and will need replacing.

However, if your power supply *is* functioning, then you have one of three potential problems. Either the monitor, the motherboard or the graphics system is faulty.

Monitor

At the risk of stating the obvious, do check that the brightness control hasn't simply been turned down inadvertently.

The first and easiest of these possibilities to rule out is the monitor. Firstly, look to see if the monitor's power light is on. If it isn't then it isn't getting any power. Check the mains supply and also the fuse in the mains lead plug.

Many newer monitors automatically initially display a message or splash screen of some sort when switched on, to show they are working. Check the manual to see if this is the case with yours. If it is then you can easily tell if the monitor is faulty or not.

Advanced Power Management is a Windows application that can cause a monitor to appear to be 'dead'. Always check this possibility first.

A common cause of a seemingly deceased monitor is a Windows application called *Advanced Power Management (APM)*. This allows the user to set a time, after which specific parts of the computer are placed in standby mode. In the case of a monitor this has the effect of blanking the screen. In theory a slight movement of the mouse will bring the monitor back to life but it doesn't always work like that. Sometimes it can take a considerable amount of mouse clicking and key bashing to get the monitor back again. Make sure this isn't the cause of the problem before going any further. If necessary reboot the PC.

Monitors carry high voltages which can be lethal. These voltages will remain until discharged – make sure they aren't discharged through you. It's obviously possible to open up a dud monitor and locate the specific fault, assuming you have the knowledge and requisite test equipment but if you don't, quite apart from wasting your time, you'll be literally risking your life and invalidating any existing guarantee. Always take a defective monitor to a repair shop.

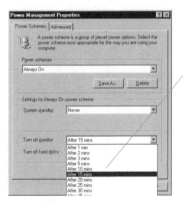

To check that an APM scheme hasn't been inadvertently enabled on your PC, right-click the *Desktop*, click *Properties, Screensavers, Settings*. From here you can alter the APM settings or turn them off completely

The next step is to substitute the monitor with one known to be good. This is the only really conclusive test.

Having ruled out the monitor you are now left with two possibilities – either the graphics card or the motherboard is faulty. This takes us into the realm of *beep codes*.

Beep Codes

The BIOS chip has an inbuilt diagnostic system whereby it alerts you to any problems it encounters during bootup. It does this in two ways – a series of coded beeps if the problem occurs before the graphics system has initialised or a text error message if the fault comes after.

You can get your BIOS details as follows: Restart the PC and after a few seconds, right at the top of the screen, you will see a brief message along the lines of 'AWARD BIOS v4.51PG'. This is the manufacturer –Award – followed by the model identification number. Obviously this will be different from PC to PC.

The procedure for eliminating the motherboard and the graphics card is essentially the same – what you must do is to listen to the PC and see if it is telling you anything in the form of any unusual noises. If it is, you will hear an irregular pattern of beeps – known as beep codes. These are produced by the BIOS chip.

If you *are* getting beep codes then you will need to know what the various codes mean. The different BIOS chip manufacturers all use different codes so first you will need to find out who the maker of your chip is.

This is easy – reboot your PC and after a few seconds you will see your BIOS details at the top of the screen. You'll have to be quick though – they don't stay there for long.

Windows ME users can also get their BIOS details by going to *Start, Programs, Accessories, System Tools.* Click *System Information* and look under *System Summary.*

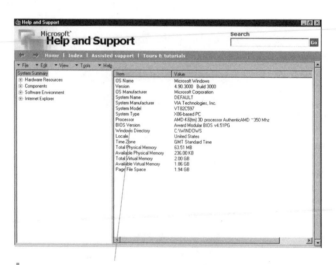

BIOS manufacturer & model no.

The three main BIOS manufacturers are AWARD, AMI & PHOENIX.

For details of these manufacturers' beep codes refer to the list at the end of this chapter.

Motherboard

The motherboard is just about the only system component that is not easy to replace. In some cases you might have to virtually take the PC apart just to get at it. They also require a considerable amount of setting up. For these reasons you are well advised to have a motherboard changed by an expert.

The motherboard is literally the heart of your system and as such is a complicated piece of circuitry. Every single part of your system is hooked up to this board. You will find there are several different codes relating to the motherboard, indicating specific problems with it such as the memory or CPU for example. These types of fault can often be repaired by replacing or reseating the associated chips and aren't necessarily too big a disaster.

However, there is also the possibility of not getting any beep codes at all and this almost always means an outright failure of the motherboard. You will usually find that the keyboard lights are not working either. In this unhappy circumstance, you'll just have to bite the bullet and get the motherboard replaced. Look on it as an opportunity to upgrade your PC, it might make you feel a bit better.

NOTE: One beep when the PC is switched on is normal and indicates that the BIOS has found no problems.

One beep when the PC is switched on is normal and indicates that all is well. Any other sequence or combination indicates that there is a problem somewhere.

Typical motherboard

Graphics Card

As with the motherboard, there are several beep codes relating to faults with graphics cards. The situation here is further complicated by the fact that some of these codes can also imply problems with the systems memory. For example, assuming you have an AWARD BIOS and are getting one long beep and two short beeps, this would indicate a probable problem with the graphics card with a less likely possibility of a fault in the memory.

All you can really do is check out the possibilities in the order of likelihood. Unfortunately, for the average PC user suspecting a fault specific to a board, the options are limited. Unless you have specialised test equipment and the knowledge to use it, you are basically restricted to the following:

It's surprising how many problems can be caused by loose or dirty connections. If you suspect your problem is hardware related, this is the first thing to check.

- Check the connections – Do this by replugging the card into its socket.

- Replacement – If you are fortunate enough to have a functional graphics card handy, perhaps from an earlier upgrade, try installing this. If you don't have another card, consider going out and buying the cheapest one you can find, as substitution is the only way to be really sure.

When checking for resource conflicts, devices to remove include sound cards, modems, TV tuner cards, printers, scanners, etc.

- Resource Conflict – You could have a situation whereby your graphics card is OK but is being prevented from working by another hardware device which is claiming the same system resources. The usual method of sorting out this type of problem is by using the *Device Manager* in the *Control Panel*. This however, requires access to Windows, which in this situation you obviously haven't got. What you've got to do therefore, is one by one, physically remove every device in the system, restarting each time and seeing if the PC now boots. If and when it does, then the last device removed will be the culprit. Once back in Windows go into the *Device Manager* to resolve the issue. Find out how to do this in the **Resource Conflict Troubleshooter**.

PC Fails to Complete Bootup

 If you are seeing an error message on the screen then you know that your graphics card is OK and that the motherboard probably is as well.

This situation is almost always accompanied by a text error message (known as a *Boot Time Error Message*) which indicates that there is at least output from the graphics card and that the motherboard is probably OK. (For an error message to be displayed the graphics system must be OK.)

The thing to do now is observe what message is on the screen when the boot procedure stops. In many cases they are self-explanatory, such as *Invalid system disk or Disk error* when you boot up with a floppy disk inserted in the floppy disk drive. Sometimes though, they can be more cryptic but will often give some indication of where the problem lies.

Invalid system disk
Replace the disk, and then press any key

 The BIOS is a chip located on the motherboard which contains all the initialisation routines required to boot the computer and then load the operating system. Instructions for accessing the BIOS setup program should be found in the BIOS setup display when booting the PC. Typically it will read 'Press ... key to enter setup'. Otherwise refer to the computer's documentation.

An error message can be produced by different parts of the system, depending on how far into the boot process the system gets before the problem occurs. Usually error messages are produced by the BIOS, as it is responsible for most of the boot procedure functions. However, other error messages are specific to the operating system and are known as *Run Time Error Messages*.

There are many thousands of individual error messages – some more common than others. However, bear in mind that since the exact wording of an error message can be changed by the manufacturer of each system, there are a lot of variations on the same theme.

Let's see what should be happening when you start the PC and also, what might not be happening. You can usually get a good clue to where the problem lies by noting exactly what stage the bootup procedure has reached before it stops.

Boot Procedure

- The first thing you should see on bootup is the BIOS message containing the name of the graphics card and its memory capacity. This indicates the card is being initialised and is working well enough to at least display simple text. If bootup stops at this point then the problem is most likely to be with the graphics card.

- Next should come the BIOS startup display. Here you will see details of your BIOS chip and also what key to hit in order to enter the BIOS setup program.

- The system will now perform the memory test. If it doesn't or hangs at this stage, there is a problem with your systems memory. Proceed according to the error message that will be displayed.

- Next comes detection of *IDE devices* such as hard drives and CD-ROM/DVD drives. Problems at this stage will usually result in error messages saying the system is having trouble identifying one or more of the IDE devices. This indicates a problem with the device itself or its configuration.

- The BIOS will now attempt to identify any *Plug & Play* devices in the system. A hang up here is usually caused by an expansion card such as a modem or sound card. The card could be faulty or causing a resource conflict. Try unplugging all the cards in turn and restarting each time.

- By now the system has identified all the hardware in the system. You should now see a system configuration summary detailing all the hardware it has found.

- The BIOS will now attempt to find and load the operating system. First it will look in the floppy drive and then the hard drive. This will be indicated by lights and physical activity in the respective drives. Any failure at this stage indicates problems with the floppy or hard disk drives or their contents. If the operating system loads or begins to load then the hardware part of the boot process has been successful.

Manufacturers' Beep Codes

As has already been stated the three main suppliers of BIOS chips are Award, AMI and Phoenix.

Award

This manufacturer's beep codes are somewhat unspecific. However for what they're worth, they are as follows:

One long beep – This indicates a memory fault, usually just a physical problem such as an incorrectly inserted module, but may also mean a bad memory chip in a module. It is also possible that there is a failure related to the motherboard or a system device.

One long, then two short beeps – This is usually caused by a problem with the graphics card or possibly the systems memory. It can also be a motherboard issue.

Continuous beeping – The system is producing constant beeping in no specific pattern. This is usually caused by a problem with the system memory, or possibly the graphics card.

AMI

Two beeps – This indicates a problem with your memory chips. Reseat them and reboot. If this doesn't work you may have a faulty chip.

Three beeps – As above.

Four beeps – As above.

Five beeps – You have a faulty motherboard.

Six beeps – The chip on your motherboard that controls your keyboard is faulty.

Seven beeps – Your CPU is faulty.

Eight beeps – The graphics card is faulty.

Nine beeps – The BIOS chip is faulty and will need replacing.

CMOS stands for Complementary Metal Oxide Semiconductor. The CMOS memory is used to store information needed for bootup.

Ten beeps – You have a problem with the CMOS. All chips associated with the CMOS will probably have to be replaced. Your may need a new motherboard.

Phoenix

Phoenix beep codes are more detailed than the AMI and Award codes. The chip emits three sets of beeps, each set being separated by a brief pause.

1-1-3 – Your computer can't read the configuration information stored in the CMOS.

1-1-4 – The BIOS chip is faulty.

1-2-1 – You have a bad timer chip on the motherboard.

1-2-2 – The motherboard is faulty.

1-2-3 – As above.

1-3-1 – As above.

1-3-3 – As above.

1-3-4 – As above.

1-4-1 – As above.

1-4-2 – You have a memory problem.

3-2-4 – The keyboard controller is faulty.

3-3-4 – Your graphics card is faulty.

4-2-1 – The motherboard is faulty.

4-3-1 – As above.

Startup Troubleshooter

Assuming the bootup procedure has gone as it should, you are still only half way to getting your PC operational. The next stage is to get Windows running and it's at this point that many problems are encountered. This chapter investigates the types of fault you are likely to get and how to overcome them. Because there are so many different reasons why Windows might refuse to run, space limitation precludes coverage of every possible fault but following the procedures outlined in this chapter should get you going ninety-nine times out of a hundred.

Covers

Windows Refuses to Start | 26

Safe Mode | 27

Windows Won't Start in Safe Mode | 28

Windows Setup | 31

Windows Starts in Safe Mode | 32

Startup Programs | 34

Resource Conflicts | 35

Re-install Windows | 36

Chapter Three

Windows Refuses to Start

The boot procedure has proceeded as it should and Windows has loaded or starts to load. However this doesn't necessarily mean Windows is going to work. You might get a *General Protection Fault*, for example, or a *Windows Protection Error*.

The process of loading the operating system (Windows in most cases) is the stage at which many problems occur.

Sometimes, for whatever reason, Windows just won't start, or won't start completely. You may get an error message as above, a blue screen *Fatal Exception error*, or you may see almost nothing at all, just the cursor flickering uselessly at the top or bottom of a black screen. No matter how many times you reboot the result is the same.

The first rule here is don't lose your cool. There may be, and often is, a simple solution. For example, there is a good possibility that the last time you exited Windows you didn't do it properly, i.e. *Start>Shutdown* or *Start>Restart*. Instead, you may have done one of the following:

- Pressed *Ctrl+Alt+Del*.

- Hit the *reset* button.

- Switched the computer off with the *on/off* button.

Many problems are caused by exiting Windows in the wrong way. Sometimes it's inevitable but wherever possible do it correctly.

- Crashed the computer.

Make a point of exiting Windows correctly

Windows reacts differently to all these 'exits'. The first one is safe enough but the other three can corrupt the system if the hard drive is being written to at the time.

Exiting Windows properly can often cure this type of problem. So try this first. The question is, how can you switch off properly if you can't get into Windows in the first place?

Safe Mode

The answer is to start Windows in *Safe Mode*. This is Windows' troubleshooting mode and the procedure bypasses the normal configuration and instead loads a minimal set of basic drivers. This eliminates a number of potential causes of the problem and will usually get you back into Windows from where you can find and fix the error.

 Safe Mode is Windows' main troubleshooting aid and works by bypassing many of Windows' usual startup files and drivers. Using Safe Mode will usually get you back into Windows from where you can carry out diagnostic tests, alter incorrect settings and effect repairs.

To do it, restart the PC and hold down the *Control* key (Windows 95 – F8) until you see the *Startup* menu. Here you will see several options.

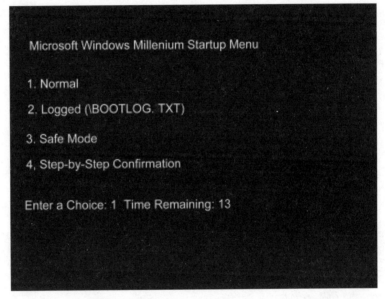

```
Microsoft Windows Millenium Startup Menu

1. Normal

2. Logged (\BOOTLOG. TXT)

3. Safe Mode

4, Step-by-Step Confirmation


Enter a Choice: 1  Time Remaining: 13
```

 When your computer is operating in Safe Mode, it will run much slower than normal. You will also find many of its functions are disabled.

Select the *Safe Mode* option and press *Enter*. With a bit of luck Windows will now start allowing you to exit properly. There's a good chance that on rebooting, Windows will load and run as normal.

NOTE: When in *Safe Mode*, Windows runs a lot slower than usual and many of its functions are disabled.

Windows Won't Start in Safe Mode

If you are unlucky and Windows won't start in *Safe Mode* either, you probably have one of the following:

- a problem with the hard drive

- a corrupted file system

- a corrupt registry

- corrupted or missing system files

- a resource conflict

- a virus

The first four faults in this list can be resolved by using your *Startup Disk*. This is one of your most important troubleshooting tools and should have been supplied by your computer supplier. If it wasn't, then make one now. Do it by going to *Control Panel, Add/Remove Programs.*

The Startup Disk doesn't restart you with Windows. Rather you will be taken into DOS, which is an alternative and more basic operating system. DOS does however, give you limited access to the system, sufficient to run diagnostic tests and carry out some repair procedures.

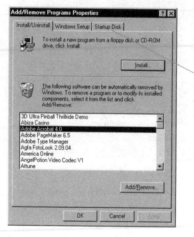

Click *Startup Disk* and then follow the instructions

Why is it so important? Because it contains all the files needed to start Windows plus a set of diagnostic tools to enable you to troubleshoot all manner of problems.

You should be aware though that the *Startup Disk* doesn't take you into Windows but rather to a DOS prompt from where you can run your diagnostics and replace any missing system files.

Place the *Startup Disk* in the floppy drive and restart the PC. You will then see a menu with various options depending on which version of Windows you are running. Option two is *Start Computer Without CD-ROM Support*. Select this option and hit *Enter*.

 Hard drives are usually labelled 'C'.
If for whatever reason, your hard drive has a different letter, e.g. 'D', then you would enter this letter when running utilities from the DOS prompt.
For example, when running *ScanDisk* you would type *SCANDISK D:* rather than *SCANDISK C:*

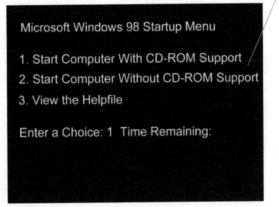

Microsoft Windows 98 Startup Menu

1. Start Computer With CD-ROM Support
2. Start Computer Without CD-ROM Support
3. View the Helpfile

Enter a Choice: 1 Time Remaining:

When you see the A:\> prompt, you are ready to go. First, run *ScanDisk* to repair any drive or file system errors by typing SCANDISK C: at the prompt

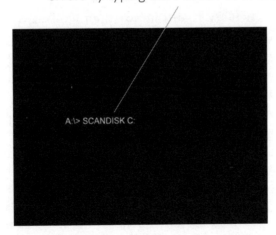

A:\> SCANDISK C:

This utility does a physical check on your drive looking for damaged sectors etc. It also examines the integrity of the file system. *ScanDisk* will repair any errors it finds.

Next, check out the *registry*. The registry is basically the heart of the operating system – every single change you make to your computer is recorded here. Making alterations to it that you shouldn't, intentional or otherwise, can have dire effects on your PC. Fortunately Windows makes automatic backups of the registry which gives you a way out of the problem. Proceed as follows:

Remember if you restore your registry to one saved on a previous date, any programs you have installed from that date will no longer run. You will need to re-install them.

- At the command prompt type: SCANREG/RESTORE. Press *Enter* then select the previous day's registry and hit *Enter* again. What you are doing is altering the registry settings to those taken on a day when the registry was known to be OK. It does mean however that any software or hardware installed after this date will need to be installed again.

- Then replace any system files that may be missing or damaged by typing SYS C: at the prompt. This will transfer the necessary files from the *Startup Disk* to the hard drive.

After each of the above steps, restart the PC and see if Windows starts normally.

If there is still no joy then you really do have an awkward problem. For example, there could be a resource conflict with your hardware. Conflicts are resolved in Windows *Device Manager* but as you cannot get into Windows, you can't access *Device Manager*.

New viruses are emerging all the time. For this reason anti-virus programs can only be relied upon if they are updated on a regular basis. This can be done by downloading updates from the manufacturer's web site.

The only other way to eliminate this possibility is to physically remove as much of the systems hardware as possible, with the exception of the graphics card and motherboard. Take out all expansion cards such as modems, sound cards, SCSI cards, etc. Disconnect printers, scanners and any other peripherals. Then reboot. If Windows now loads, then one of the devices was causing the problem. Re-install them individually, rebooting each time, until you have located the faulty device.

There is also the chance of virus infection. An anti-virus program will check this, but make sure it is up to date.

Windows Setup

If Windows still won't go you will have to run *Windows Setup* again. This will replace any files that are missing or corrupted and should sort out any resource conflicts. It's quite simple to do.

Insert your Windows CD-ROM, and then using the *Startup Disk*, select option one – *Start Computer With CD-ROM Support*. Hit *Enter*

Note that the Startup Disk will shift your CD-ROM drive letter up one, i.e. if it was 'D', it will now be 'E'.

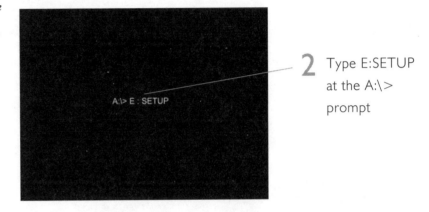

A:\> E : SETUP

2 Type E:SETUP at the A:\> prompt

Make sure you have your Microsoft product key available before you attempt to install Windows. You will find this on the back of the CD case or sleeve.

Windows will now install itself over the existing installation. This will take 30 to 40 minutes to complete. All you need to do is ensure that you have your Windows CD product number handy.

If you *still* cannot get Windows to run after this, then your system is well and truly screwed up. Your only option now is a *clean* installation of Windows. What this means is that the hard drive is literally wiped clean of everything that was previously on it, including whatever problem was preventing Windows from running.

The procedure for doing this is known as *Formatting*. When Windows is installed on to a clean drive, you will find that not only has your PC come back to life, but it will also run like new. For instructions on how to do a clean installation go to the end of this troubleshooter.

Windows Starts in Safe Mode

If however, you can get into Windows via *Safe Mode* then the first thing to check is the AUTOEXEC.BAT, CONFIG.SYS, WIN.INI and SYSTEM.INI. files.

These files date back to the early days of Windows, when they were important files that told DOS and Windows, amongst other things, which programs to load when a computer was switched on. With the introduction of Windows 98, ME, 2000 and XP, this role was largely eliminated and these files are now used mainly to provide backward compatibility to older programs and applications. However in certain circumstances they can interfere with the successful loading of Windows. If you find that bypassing these files results in Windows loading correctly, it means one of them has become corrupted. Check them out as follows:

Procedure for Windows 98 & ME
Click *Start, Run*.

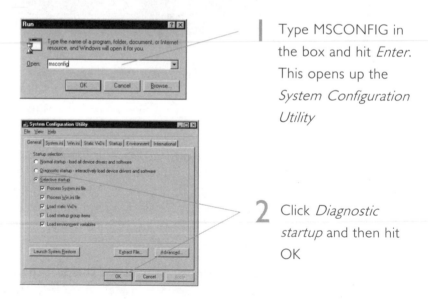

I Type MSCONFIG in the box and hit *Enter*. This opens up the *System Configuration Utility*

2 Click *Diagnostic startup* and then hit OK

Reboot the PC. Hold down the *Control* key until you see the *Startup Menu*. Choose *Step By Step Confirmation*. When you are prompted to process the AUTOEXEC.BAT and CONFIG.SYS files, press the *Esc* key to bypass them. Hit *Enter* to load everything else. If Windows starts normally now then an entry in one of these files is causing the problem. It must either be removed or corrected. This is a straightforward enough procedure but somewhat long-winded to describe. For instructions on how to do it refer to the *Windows Startup Troubleshooter* which can be located by going to *Start, Help* and then typing *Troubleshooting* in the box. In the drop down list, scroll down to *startup* and click *Display*.

Windows provides some excellent faultfinding tips in its series of troubleshooters. You can access these by going to Start and then clicking Help.

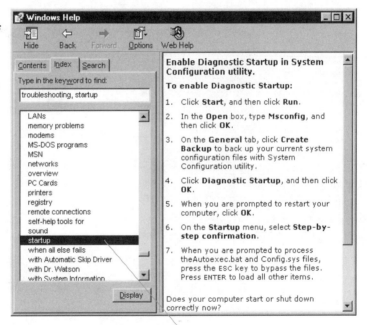

Select the *Startup* troubleshooter by clicking here

Users of Windows 95 will get the System Configuration Editor rather than the System Configuration Utility when they type SYSEDIT in the Run box.

Procedure for Windows 95

The procedure is exactly the same with one exception. Instead of a *System Configuration Utility*, Windows 95 comes with a *System Configuration Editor*. Click *Start, Run* and type SYSEDIT in the box. Then proceed as per Windows 98 & ME.

Startup Programs

If Windows still won't run, then try this next: Go to *Start, Settings, Taskbar and Start Menu.* Click *Advanced* then click *Advanced* again. Click the (+) sign next to *Programs.* Click the *StartUp* folder. Move all the icons now revealed to a different folder. These icons represent the programs which load automatically with Windows. Reboot. If Windows loads OK now then one of the programs is faulty and was preventing Windows from running. Isolate the culprit by moving the icons one by one back into the *StartUp* folder, rebooting each time until Windows refuses to load again. Then either remove the program or re-install it.

Another way of accessing the StartUp folder is by going to Start, Programs and clicking StartUp.

1 Click + sign next to *Programs*	2 Click the *StartUp* folder	3 These icons represent the programs which automatically start with Windows. Move all of them to a different folder

Resource Conflicts

The Device Manager provides a very easy way of eliminating your hardware devices if you suspect they could be causing a problem. Simply tick the Disable In This Hardware Profile box for each device you wish to eliminate.

If the *StartUp* programs are OK you could have a problem with resource conflicts or damaged/corrupted device drivers. Check these as follows:

Go into *Control Panel, System, Device Manager*, and check that your device drivers are installed and that there are no resource conflicts reported. (See Chapter Eleven.)

Next, click the *General* tab and disable the following devices by clicking the *Disable In This Hardware Profile* check box for each.

- Display adapters

- Floppy disk controllers

- Hard disk controllers

- Keyboard

- Mouse

- Network adapters

- Ports (COM & LPT)

- SCSI controllers

- Sound, video, and game controllers

Restart the PC in *Safe Mode* and one by one, re-enable the devices, restarting the computer each time. In this way you will discover if any of your systems hardware devices are causing the problem and if so, which. Correcting this type of problem usually means re-installing the drivers for the device in question.

If the operating system still won't run properly, the odds are you have a damaged or corrupted registry which will need repairing. Do this by running SCANREG/RESTORE as already described.

Re-install Windows

When doing a 'clean' installation of Windows as opposed to a re-installation, all data on the drive will be permanently erased.

Therefore any data you don't wish to lose must be backed up first to a different drive or media.

If, after all of this, you still cannot get Windows to load normally, the last option open to you is to do a clean re-installation of Windows itself. This isn't as big a deal as some people like to make out. You must remember though that the *Format* procedure which prepares the hard drive for the new installation, will wipe the drive clean. In other words all your programs and data will be lost.

Therefore before you embark on this little adventure you must create a backup copy of any data you wish to keep. Don't forget things like your *Address Book* and the contents of your *Favorites* folder.

To re-install Windows do the following:

- Insert your *Startup Disk* and select option one.

- Place your Windows CD in the CD-ROM drive.

While a clean installation of Windows isn't as difficult as many people think, it's essential that you understand the procedures involved (e.g. formatting). You must also ensure that you have a CD-ROM boot floppy disk. This allows you to access your CD-ROM drive which will be needed for the Windows installation CD.

- At the A:\> prompt type FORMAT C: where C is your hard drive. This process will take between 30 minutes and an hour depending on the size of your hard drive.

- When the format is finished, you will be returned to the A:\> prompt. Type E:SETUP and hit *Enter*. Windows setup will begin and all you have to do is follow the on-screen instructions.

Note: Before you format your hard drive make sure you have a CD-ROM boot floppy disk. This should have been provided by your computer supplier and will contain drivers for your CD-ROM drive. Depending on what model of CD-ROM drive you have in your system, you may need this disk during the above procedure.

This applies particularly to users of Windows 95. Those of you running Windows 98/ME/XP already have a boot floppy in the form of your *Startup Disk* which contains generic CD-ROM drivers.

Just make sure that you have made a *Startup Disk*.

Shutdown Troubleshooter

It's not uncommon for Windows users to find that their PC hangs when they attempt to shut it down. There are numerous causes for this and by working your way through this troubleshooter you will soon isolate the problem.

Covers

Fast Shutdown (Win 98 Only) | 38

Exit Sound File | 39

Temporary Folders | 40

Windows Initialisation Files | 41

Startup Programs | 43

Advanced Power Management | 44

Chapter Four

Fast Shutdown (Win 98 Only)

There is a well documented bug with Windows 98 2nd Edition, whereby having the *Fast Shutdown* feature enabled causes the computer to hang when you attempt to close it down. To establish whether this is the case you must disable the feature.

If your PC hangs during shutdown and you are running Windows 98 2nd edition, the most likely cause is the Fast Shutdown feature. Disable it and then try again.

Do this by going to *Start, Run* and typing MSCONFIG in the box. Click OK and then click *Advanced*. Place a check mark in the box next to *Disable fast shutdown*. Click OK, then OK again.

If Windows shuts down now then you know the *Fast Shutdown* feature was causing the problem. You now have two choices: either leave the feature permanently disabled or obtain a workaround patch from the Microsoft web site (www.microsoft.com/windows98/downloads/corporate.asp).

You can obtain a patch for this problem by visiting the Microsoft web site at 'www.microsoft.com/ windows98/downloads/ corporate.asp'

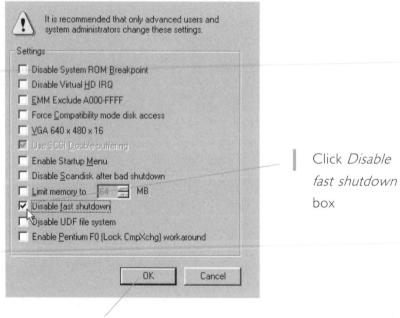

Click *Disable fast shutdown* box

2 Click OK

Exit Sound File

Windows provides any number of sounds. Many people run a PC for years using the default sounds, never realising they have a choice.

If the sound file that is used by Windows when it shuts down has become corrupted, it can prevent the PC from shutting down.

Check this out as follows:

| Go to *Control Panel* and click *Sounds*

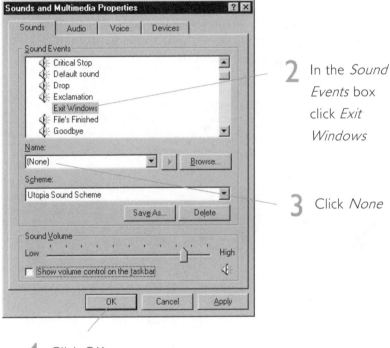

2 In the *Sound Events* box click *Exit Windows*

3 Click *None*

4 Click OK

Now shut down Windows. If Windows does not hang, the problem was a corrupt sound file. All you have to do is to simply re-install the sound file in question or select a different one.

Temporary Folders

Installing/uninstalling applications, running programs and browsing the web, all result in the PC placing temporary files in various folders on your hard drive. If these files are not periodically cleared out they can accumulate to an alarming degree and literally clog up your computer.

Surfing the web can cause your Temporary Internet Files folder to fill up at an alarming rate, particularly if you are browsing graphics rich sites. Make a point of clearing it out every now and again.

One possible result of this is improper shutdown of Windows. Open your hard drive and have a look in the *Temp* folder and the *Temporary Internet Files* folder, both in the Windows folder. The odds are they will be stuffed to the gills with all sorts of rubbish. Delete the lot, none of it is of any importance.

Bulging 'Temporary' folders can have other adverse effects on your computer. System instability is one such.

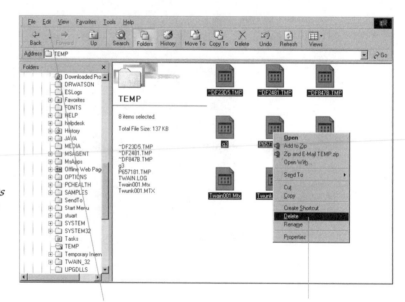

1 Click *Select All* in the *Edit* menu

2 Right-click and hit *Delete*

Windows Initialisation Files

The AUTOEXEC.BAT and CONFIG.SYS files are basically a set of commands that are carried out when a PC is started or restarted. Corruption of either can prevent proper shutdown. This possibility can be checked by configuring the computer to start without loading these files. This is done as follows:

If you are running Windows 95, then you must type SYSEDIT in the Open box. This will take you to the System Configuration Editor. This is simply 95's version of the System Configuration Utility. The rest of the procedure remains the same.

1 Click *Start* and then click *Run*

2 In the *Open* box, type MSCONFIG, then click OK

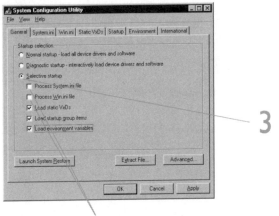

3 Click *Selective startup*

4 Clear the *Process System.ini file* and *Process Win.ini file* check boxes, and then click OK

5 Reboot the computer

If it starts and shuts down correctly now there is a problem with an entry in one or other of these files. To find out which one, do the following:

1 Carry out steps 1 to 2 as above

2 Click the *System.ini* tab

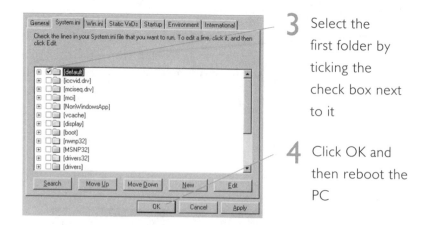

3 Select the first folder by ticking the check box next to it

4 Click OK and then reboot the PC

5 Repeat the last four steps for each folder on the tab, until your computer refuses to shut down. The last folder to be selected is the culprit

6 Clear the check box next to this folder, click the folder to display the entries within it, and then repeat steps 1 through 4 again for each entry in the folder. When your computer fails to shut down correctly, you will know that the last entry you selected is responsible for the error

If the *System.ini* files appear to be OK, then repeat the whole procedure with the *Win.ini* files. If and when you discover that a particular entry is causing the problem, then simply leave that entry turned off.

Turn the other entries in both the *System.ini* and *Win.ini* folders back on and then reboot the PC.

You then have the choice of either leaving the faulty entry disabled or contacting the manufacturer of the driver or device mentioned in the entry for advice.

Startup Programs

On the hard drive there exists a folder called the *Startup* folder. Any programs in this folder start automatically with Windows. Problems with any of these applications can lead to shutdown errors. To establish if this is indeed what's happening do the following:

Go to *Start, Settings, Taskbar* and *Start Menu*. Click the *Advanced* tab and in the next dialog box click *Advanced* again. Click the + sign next to *Programs* and then click the *StartUp* folder. In the right hand pane you will now see revealed icons, each one of which represents a program which automatically starts when Windows is loaded.

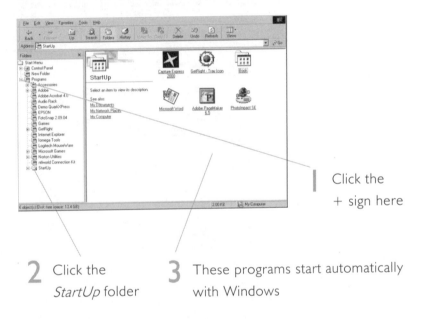

Click the
+ sign here

2 Click the *StartUp* folder

3 These programs start automatically with Windows

All you have to do is create another folder and drag the startup programs to it. Now reboot the PC and if it now shuts down OK, you know one of the startup programs was causing the problem. One by one, drag them back to the *StartUp* folder, rebooting each time. When the PC refuses to shut down, the last program dragged to the *StartUp* folder will be the culprit. Either delete or re-install it.

Advanced Power Management

Advanced Power Management can also be turned off in the BIOS setup program which can be accessed by rebooting and pressing the Delete key. However this step is only recommended for experienced users familiar with the BIOS. Incorrect settings here can mess your system up completely.

APM is a relatively new concept that can cause a host of seemingly unrelated problems. One area in which it can have an effect is the correct shutting down of Windows. This can be checked by simply turning it off.

Do this as follows:

1 Go to *Control Panel, System, Device Manager, System Devices, Advanced Power Management Support, Properties*

2 Tick the *Disable in this hardware profile* check box

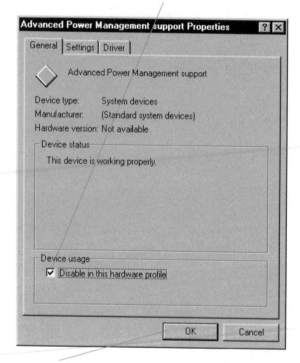

3 Click OK

4 Restart the PC. If the PC shuts down OK now then either leave APM disabled or seek further advice

Windows Setup Troubleshooter

Installing a new version or re-installing an existing version of Windows is, in theory, a pretty straightforward procedure. You really don't have to do anything much other than sit there drinking tea and clicking OK now and again – usually.

However, it doesn't always go according to plan. There are in fact many things which can go wrong. These can range from the serious such as crashes/hangs to simply losing a setting or two from the previous setup.

The vast majority of the problems associated with Windows installations are a result of users not taking a few simple precautions before beginning.

This chapter will show you how to achieve a trouble free Windows installation.

Covers

Preparation | 46

Setup Fails | 47

Clean Installation | 48

Setup Error Messages | 49

Chapter Five

Preparation

A clean Windows installation will wipe your hard drive clean of all previously stored data. So before you start make sure you have backed up all data that you don't wish to lose. This can be done on a second hard drive, floppy/ Zip disks or a rewriteable CD.

There are several considerations to take into account before you get started, depending on what you are planning to do. For example you may be upgrading an existing version. On the other hand you could be doing a clean installation, i.e. installing onto a newly formatted hard drive.

If you're doing a clean installation, you must make backups of any data you don't wish to lose. Don't forget things like your email address book and Internet Favorites. Go through the hard drive methodically and make a copy of everything you want to keep. If you just backup the things you can think of, you will be surprised later on (when it's too late) at the number of things you didn't think of. You *must* also have a bootable floppy disk to hand, i.e. a floppy disk containing the driver for your CD-ROM drive. If you haven't, you might not be able to access the CD-ROM drive and hence you won't be able to load Windows. This applies particularly to users of Windows 95.

Windows 98 and ME Startup Disks have CD-ROM driver support built in, so if you are running either of these, you needn't worry about a bootable disk. You already have one.

Make sure your hard drive is in good order by running *ScanDisk* and *Disk Defragmenter*. Any problems here can halt the installation. NOTE: The version of *ScanDisk* run during Windows Setup only checks for errors. It does not fix them. If there are problems, Setup will not be able to continue until they are fixed. Therefore run *ScanDisk* before you start.

Run a virus check on your system. In the unlikely event of you having a virus it would be rather silly to transfer it to your new setup. Also make sure you have no anti-virus programs running. These can cause all sorts of setup problems.

Disable any programs that run in the background and suddenly activate, such as screensavers, virus checkers and utility programs. It's also a good idea to remove all programs in the *StartUp* folder.

If you carry out all of the above steps it's almost certain that Windows will install itself without a hitch. If however it doesn't, you may well experience any of the following problems:

Setup Fails

A common mistake that people make is to try and install Windows with an anti-virus program running in the background. This is likely to cause problems. Make sure that you disable or uninstall these programs before you start.

You're sitting there watching the Setup progress bar creeping inexorably forward and wondering what all the fuss is about, when without warning it stops. Now, suddenly, you know.

Usually in this situation, you will get an error message. Windows has a host of these messages to help you out when things go wrong. What action you take obviously depends on what the message is telling you. Some of them will tell you nothing at all such as *Error SU8079 – An unknown error occurred*. Many, however, will tell you the exact nature of the problem and what to do about it. A good example is: *Error SU0014 – Setup has found a hardware device on your computer that is not responding. To try this device again, click Continue. If problems persist, quit Setup and any other running programs, and then turn your computer off and back on again. Then run Setup again, and choose Safe Recovery when prompted.*

If the error message doesn't make sense or you don't know how to do what it's telling you to do, try the following:

Windows Setup includes a feature called *Safe Recovery*. This is the first thing to try. Restart the PC and run Setup again. When given the option select *Safe Recovery*. This utility will resume the installation by missing out the step that caused Setup to hang. If you choose not to use it then Setup starts again from the beginning.

The best way to achieve a trouble free Windows installation and avoid error messages, hangs, etc., is to follow the procedures in the *Preparation* section of this troubleshooter.

Make a note of what stage Setup has reached when it stops. This will provide a good clue. During the installation Windows keeps you advised of what it is doing, i.e. copying files, detecting your system hardware, etc. The latter is a common cause of problems and is usually caused by a resource conflict. See Chapter Eleven on how to deal with this.

If, however, Setup hangs regardless of what you do, then it's time to get your *Startup Disk* out. Select option one and when you see the DOS prompt, type E: SETUP and hit *Enter*. Without going into the reasons, installing from DOS will often get an installation to run whereas it wouldn't from within Windows.

Clean Installation

If you can't get Setup to run even from the DOS prompt then you will have no choice but to do a clean installation. You must remember though that this procedure will wipe your hard drive completely, so any data that you don't wish to lose must be backed up before you proceed any further.

Do a clean installation of Windows as follows:

1. Insert your *Startup Disk* and select option one – *Start Computer With CD-ROM Support*. After a few seconds, you will see the following DOS screen

Without any doubt, the best way to install Windows is to do a clean installation. The reason this is so is because you must first format the drive which wipes it clean. This also wipes out any potential problems waiting to interfere with the installation.

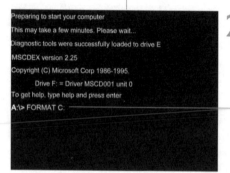

```
Preparing to start your computer
This may take a few minutes. Please wait...
Diagnostic tools were successfully loaded to drive E
MSCDEX version 2.25
Copyright (C) Microsoft Corp 1986-1995.
          Drive F: = Driver MSCD001 unit 0
To get help, type help and press enter
A:\> FORMAT C:
```

2. Place your Windows CD in the CD-ROM drive. At the A:\> prompt type FORMAT C: where C is your hard drive. Hit *Enter*. You will now see the following message

```
Warning, all data on non-removeable disk
Drive C: will be lost!
Proceed with format (Y/N)?
```

3. Hit the letter Y and then *Enter*. Formatting will now proceed. This process will take about 30 minutes to an hour depending on the size of your hard drive and speed of your computer

When the format is finished, you will be returned to the A:\> prompt. Type E:SETUP and hit *Enter*. Windows Setup will begin and all you have to do is follow the on-screen instructions.

Setup Error Messages

If you are planning to do a clean installation using an upgrade version of Windows, make sure you have the original full version to hand before you format your hard drive.

The reason for this is that Windows will detect that you are using an upgrade version and insist on seeing a full version before continuing.

If you are unable to produce one for whatever reason, you will be left with an empty formatted drive and no way to load Windows. You will then have no alternative but to go out and buy a full version of Windows.

The following is a list of the more common error messages you are likely to see ('X' is a replaceable parameter):

SU0014 – Setup has found a hardware device on your computer that is not responding. To try this device again, click *Continue*. If problems persist, quit Setup and any other running programs, and then turn your computer off and back on again. Then run Setup again, and choose *Safe Recovery* when prompted.

SU0018 – Setup could not create files on your startup drive and cannot set up Windows. There may be too many files in the root directory of your startup drive, or your startup drive letter may have been remapped by network or compression software. For more information, see SETUP.TXT on Setup Disk 1 or the Windows CD-ROM.

SU0019 – Setup has found commands in your AUTOEXEC.BAT or CONFIG.SYS files that are not compatible with Windows. Setup will make backup copies of your existing AUTOEXEC.BAT and CONFIG.SYS files and create new ones, if needed.

SU0129 – Setup was unable to determine your computer's hardware configuration. Setup cannot continue and will now close.

SU0133 – Setup was unable to determine your system configuration by using full detection. Would you like to try again using minimal detection?
Note: If this doesn't work, run Setup again and choose *Safe Recovery* when prompted.

SU0135 – Setup was unable to properly identify all your hardware. To confirm your hardware settings, click *Change Computer Settings.*

SU0136 – Setup was unable to initialize Windows *Help*. *Help* may not be available during Windows Setup.

SU0141 – Setup could not copy files needed for your startup disk. You can still continue with Setup without creating the startup disk. Click OK to continue.

If you are upgrading over an existing version of Windows and can spare about 200MB hard drive space, a good idea is to copy the Windows Setup files from the CD to a new folder on your drive. You can then run Setup directly from your hard drive, which has several advantages.

Setup will be quicker, you won't damage your Windows CD and if Windows subsequently asks you to put your CD in the CD-ROM drive for some reason, all you have to do is point Windows to the folder containing the Setup files.

SU0147 – Setup did not find enough free directory entries in the root of your startup drive. Please delete some files or directories to make enough room, and then run Setup again. Setup needs at least X more free entries on this drive.

SU0151 – Setup could not verify that your computer has the minimum amount of memory (RAM) required to run Windows 95 (or Windows 98). Do you want to continue with Setup?

SU0153 – Drive X, the host drive for the compressed X drive, must have at least X bytes free to set up Windows. Free some disk space, and then run Setup again.

SU0161 – The directory X which is needed to install Windows into already contains a Windows installation. Setup will choose a directory for you, which you can change later.

SU0168 – Your computer already has an operating system installed, which cannot be upgraded by this version of Setup.

SU0335 – Setup could not determine your hardware settings. There may be a missing or damaged Setup file or there may not be enough memory to continue. Free some memory and then run Setup again.

SU0362 – It is not recommended that Setup continue without the proper amount of disk space free. If you continue, Setup may run out of disk space and not complete successfully.

SU0404 – Setup is already running.

SU0409 – Windows Setup was unable to update your system files. This may be caused by virus detection that is built in to your computer, or by virus detection software running on your computer.

Hard Drive Troubleshooter

The modern day hard drive is a wonderful piece of kit, not just because of its enormous storage capacity and reliability, but also because of the incredibly fine tolerances to which it is built. When you consider that the distance between the read/write heads and the storage disks is less than the thickness of a human hair and that the heads are moving constantly over a period of years, the fact that it *is* so reliable is even more remarkable.

Having said all that, it's not unknown for them to fail and when they do, it's usually terminal. Hard drives cannot usually be repaired – you simply throw them away and get a new one. Unfortunately, all the data they contain is thrown away with them and this is why you must create backup copies of any data you simply cannot afford to lose.

Covers

Hard Drive Failure | 52

Hard Drive Is Not Being Recognised | 53

Hard Drive Is Being Recognised | 54

Performance Issues | 55

New Drive Won't Boot | 59

Common Hard Drive Error Messages | 60

Chapter Six

Hard Drive Failure

Many BIOS programs are password protected. If this is the case with yours and you don't know the password then simply contact the manufacturer of your PC.

Another way of finding out if your hard drive is working OK, is by using your *Startup Disk.*

Boot to the A:/> prompt and type *DIR C:*

Hit *Enter* and if the drive is working, you will see a DOS window detailing the contents of the drive. At the bottom will be displayed the number of files and directories and the available free space.

It's not usually too difficult to spot a hard drive which has failed. Your PC will usually refuse to boot and you will almost certainly see an error message, which might or might not give you an indication of where the problem lies. However, if there isn't one or you simply can't make any sense of it, then work through the following steps:

The first thing to do is to establish whether or not the drive is being recognised by the system. To do this you must enter the BIOS setup program and see whether the drive has been detected. Do this as follows: Reboot the computer and follow the on-screen instructions for accessing the BIOS setup program, or refer to the computer's documentation.

As soon as the BIOS setup program opens you will probably see a message prompting you for a password. If you don't know what it is then you'll have to contact the manufacturer. Once in BIOS however, you will see various options, one of which will read *Standard CMOS setup*. If the BIOS *has* recognised your drive, its parameters will be listed here.

If the drive *hasn't* been recognised, then do the following: Using the arrow keys, navigate your way to *IDE HDD Auto Detection* and press *Enter*. You will see a new message asking you to *select Primary Master*. Under this you should now see the details of your drive. Hit *Enter*. Next, you will see three more screens in succession, all asking you to select *Secondary Master*, *Primary Slave* and *Secondary Slave* respectively. Keep hitting *Enter* until you are back to the original BIOS screen. Go to *Save setup and exit* and hit *Enter*. You will be asked to confirm by typing the letter Y. Do so and hit *Enter* again. Hit *Esc* and the computer will restart.

If the drive has been detected by the BIOS, it indicates that the drive itself is ok and that the problem is software related. Skip the next section and go on to **Hard Drive Is Being Recognised**. If it hasn't been detected, go to **Hard Drive Is Not Being Recognised** on the next page.

Hard Drive Is Not Being Recognised

If the BIOS does not see your drive, the odds are that you have a problem with the hard drive itself, its power supply or its connections. There is also a possibility of a boot sector virus.

A boot sector virus infects the Master Boot Record (MBR) of a drive. Since the MBR executes every time a computer is started, a boot sector virus is extremely dangerous. Once the boot code on the drive is infected, the virus will be loaded into memory on every startup. From memory the boot virus can spread to every disk that the system reads.

The latter is the first thing to rule out. Obtain an up-to-date anti-virus program and check your drive with it.

Next, you need to determine if the drive has power and is spinning up. The easiest way to do this is to take the cover off the PC and listen as you turn the power on. You should be able to hear the drive spin up. If it spins up and then spins back down again immediately, this is a sure sign of a problem with the drive unit. If it doesn't spin up at all, then either the drive is defective, or there is a problem with its power supply.

To check this, plug the hard drive's power cable into the CD-ROM drive. If the CD-ROM drive works OK, then you know that the hard drive is getting power and therefore must be faulty. Replace it with a new one.

However, out-of-the-blue failure of a hard drive is unusual. Being a mechanical device it will usually exhibit warning signs of impending failure. Things to watch out for include an unusual amount of activity, excessive noise, taking longer than usual to spin up and increasingly frequent reports from *ScanDisk* of bad sectors.

Sudden failure of a hard drive is rare. Normally a drive will display symptoms which indicate that it is on the way out. Typical indications are overheating, excessive noise and drive activity.

If you have suspicions open up the case and check the drive isn't overheating. It should be warm to hot but definitely not too hot to touch.

Most drive failures will be accompanied by an error message. Typical messages include: *Not ready reading drive, Sector not found, Error encountered initializing hard drive, Hard drive Failure.*

Hard Drive Is Being Recognised

If your drive is being recognised by the BIOS, this is a good sign that it is OK.

This isn't as serious as the previous scenario, as it indicates that the drive itself is probably OK.

Take note of any error message you may be seeing, such as *Error encountered initialising hard drive* for example. These messages can be helpful in tracking down the problem. Refer to the list of error messages at the end of this chapter.

The next thing you've got to do is gain access to the drive so that you can try and establish what the problem is and repair it. To do this you need to get your *Startup Disk* out and do the following:

If you are unable to access your hard drive via Windows, then you must use your Startup Disk. This will enable you to run diagnostic and repair utilities such as ScanDisk.

Firstly, check the drive for physical errors such as damaged sectors or for a corrupted file system. Do this by running *ScanDisk* – enter SCANDISK C: at the prompt.

Next, rule out the possibility of a boot sector virus infection by running an up-to-date anti-virus program.

Make sure your system files are intact by entering SYS C: at the prompt. This will transfer a copy of the system files needed to load Windows, to the drive. If any of these files are corrupted then Windows might refuse to run.

Check for resource conflicts. Turn off the computer and remove all the peripherals and expansion cards except for the graphics card and motherboard. Reboot and if the computer recognises the drive this time, then you know there is a conflict with one of the devices. Re-install them one at a time, rebooting each time, until the conflict re-occurs. Once you know which device is causing the problem, you can remove it, thus allowing you back into Windows from where you can resolve the problem in *Device Manager*. See **Resource Conflict Troubleshooter.**

Ninety-nine times out of a hundred, following the above steps will resolve the problem.

If however, you still cannot get the system to boot, you almost certainly have a faulty hard drive, notwithstanding the fact that it is being recognised by the system.

Performance Issues

As has already been stated hard drives are very dependable devices, which can usually be relied upon to give years of trouble free operation. However, to keep them running at peak efficiency does require a certain amount of maintenance.

Hard Drive Is Running Slowly

There are several causes of this problem, all of which are straightforward enough to put right.

Probably the most common reason is a fragmented drive. When data is written to a drive, be it a hard drive, CD-ROM or floppy drive, it is saved contiguously. However, over a period of time, as files are saved and deleted, programs installed and uninstalled, the data becomes fragmented, i.e. scattered randomly throughout the drive. This means the read/write heads have to work harder in order to find the requested data. The inevitable result of this is that the drive takes longer to perform its tasks.

This problem can be resolved by using a Windows utility called *Disk Defragmenter*. Go to *Start, Programs, Accessories, System Tools* and then click *Disk Defragmenter*. Simply select the drive you want to defragment and click OK.

Hard drive performance can be improved considerably by regular maintenance. Run ScanDisk regularly and certainly after an incorrect shutdown. Also defragment the drive every month or so by running a defragment utility.

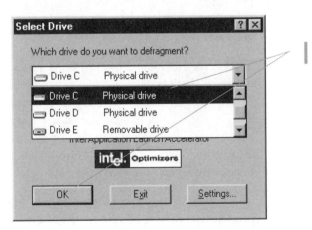

Select the drive to be defragmented and then click OK

Viruses

A virus is basically a small piece of software and can be programmed to do literally anything on a computer. One of the favourite targets for a virus writer is a PC's drives as the virus can be so easily spread from them to other parts of the computer and even to other computers.

To guard against the possibility of acquiring a virus, every computer user should invest in an anti-virus program. These come in two main categories – *Specific* and *Generic*.

If you are having problems with your hard drive, never discount the possibility that it has been infected by a virus. Drives are favourite targets for virus writers.

Generic programs work by building a database of information on every component of a computer likely to be affected by a virus. If and when the said virus strikes, the program will be able to undo any damage caused by rebuilding the affected files. As an example of how cunning they can be, they can actually 'bait' the computer by creating a file and then keeping a close watch on it to see if anything tries to access it.

Specific programs are databases which contain details of every known virus, or to put it another way, their *fingerprints*. As soon as a virus invades a PC the program spots it and alerts the user. The main problem with this method is that as soon as a new virus is written, the *Specific* type of program becomes out of date and so has to be continually updated, usually by downloading from the program manufacturer's web site.

There are literally thousands of viruses in existence, most of which will at worst cause a few minor headaches. For example you might get silly and irritating messages flashing across your screen. On the other hand there are a few which can have devastating consequences to any PC unfortunate enough to contract them. These can cause computers to crash and even wipe all the data off hard drives.

So, if your drive is misbehaving in any way, suspect the possibility that it has been infected by a virus.

Compatibility Mode

The computer may be running in *Compatibility Mode*. This situation usually occurs when a drive is operating with an incorrect or corrupted driver. The result is a slow-down in the hard drive's performance. Check this as follows:

1 Go to *Control Panel, System* and click the *Performance* tab

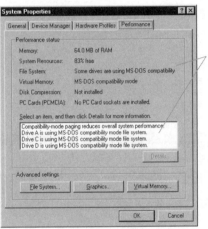

2 If you are in *Compatibility Mode* it will tell you here. If not, you will see a message saying *Your System Is Configured For Optimal Performance*

3 If you are in *Compatibility Mode* go to *Control Panel, System, Device Manager*

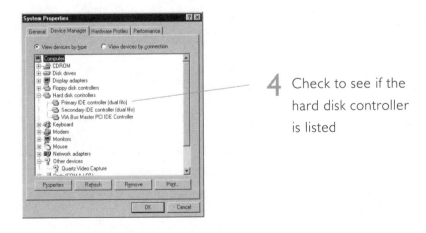

4 Check to see if the hard disk controller is listed

If the hard disk controller isn't listed then it has not been installed. Install it with the *Add New Hardware Wizard* in the *Control Panel*.

If it is listed in *Device Manager* but has a red X over it, it has been disabled. Click *Properties* and then click the check box corresponding to the current hardware profile under *Device Usage*.

If the hard disk controller has a yellow exclamation mark over it, then either there is a resource conflict with another device, the *Protected mode driver* is missing or damaged, or the *Disable all 32-bit protected-mode disk drivers* option has been selected. To access the latter, go to *System* in *Control Panel*, click the *Performance* tab, and then click *File System, Troubleshooting*.

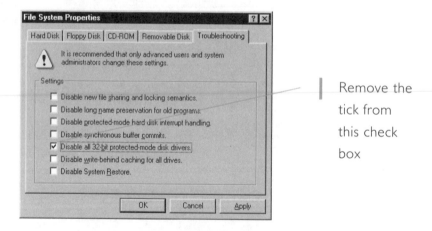

Remove the tick from this check box

Resolve any resource conflicts in *Device Manager* as described in Chapter Eleven.

To check if there is a problem with the *Protected mode driver*, click the controller in *Device Manager*, click the *Driver* tab then click *Update Driver*. Windows will now find and install the best available driver for this device.

New Drive Won't Boot

One of the most common problems is due to people not realising that before a new drive will work, it has first to be partitioned and then formatted. These procedures basically prepare the drive so it can be recognised and used by the operating system.

Partitioning & Formatting

The procedure is as follows:

When entering commands at the DOS prompt, be aware of the differences in English & American spelling. For example entering FDISC at the prompt will just return a bad command message. You must use the American spelling, i.e. FDISK.

- Insert the *Startup Disk* into the floppy drive and boot the PC.

- At the A:\> prompt type FDISK and hit *Enter*.

- The first thing you will see is a long message asking if you wish to enable large drive support. Ignore this by hitting *Enter*.

- You will now see a DOS window giving you four options. Select option one and hit *Enter*.

- In the new window that appears select option one again, which will say *Create Primary DOS Partition*. Hit *Enter*.

- You will now be given the option of how big to make your partition. This issue of partitioning is a complex one so you are advised to take the simplest option and choose a partition size of 100%. Hit *Enter* and you will be told that a *Primary DOS Partition Has Been Created*.

The partioning part of the procedure is now finished. Exit FDISK by hitting the *Esc* key and you will see the A:\> prompt again.

Now the new drive must be formatted, i.e. a folder and file structure must be created to enable Windows to use the drive.

At the prompt type FORMAT C:

After a warning message advising you that formatting will destroy all data on the drive, the formatting procedure will take place. When finished the drive will be ready for use.

Common Hard Drive Error Messages

Hard disk configuration error – This message is usually seen as the system boots up. Enter the BIOS setup program and make sure that your hard drive is set up correctly.

Hard disk failure – Usually occurs as the system boots up. Check the BIOS to make sure the hard drive is set up correctly. Check that the drive is receiving power.

Hard disk controller failure – If you see this message as the system boots up, power down the system. Check the data cable connection to the drive and also to the motherboard.

Invalid drive specification – This message indicates your hard drive has been incorrectly configured in BIOS. Check the settings and if necessary correct them. Refer to the documentation if in any doubt. If the hard drive settings are OK, the problem may be with the FDISK partition on the hard drive.

Error selecting drive – Same as above.

No boot device available – This error will show up if the boot record on the hard drive is corrupted or missing. Check for a boot sector virus, then use your *Startup Disk* to transfer a copy of the Windows system files to the drive.

A serious disk error occurred while trying to read/write drive X – This error message indicates a physical problem with the drive. Check the drive's power supply and cable connections. Also run *ScanDisk* to make sure there are no errors on the drive.

DVD/CD/Floppy Drive Troubleshooter

Although DVD/CD-ROM and floppy drives employ totally different technologies, for troubleshooting purposes they are very similar and thus will be considered the same unless otherwise stated.

Faults with the actual drive mechanisms are rare and are usually restricted to issues with accumulated dust and grime.

Most problems that occur relate to the software or media used by the device. This is because removable media is extremely susceptible to physical damage and not a few headaches are a result of careless handling.

DVD (Digital Video Disk) drives, supplied with most new systems nowadays, can cause problems due to the intense demand placed on the computer's resources.

Covers

Drive Doesn't Work | 62

CD Problems | 64

DVD Problems | 65

DVDs/CDs Don't Auto Play | 66

Floppy Disk Problems | 67

Chapter Seven

Drive Doesn't Work

Firstly, establish whether or not it is being recognised by Windows. Do this by going to *Control Panel, System, Device Manager*. If Windows can see it then it will be listed.

Faults with actual drive units are rare. Most problems are a result of damaged media – CDs, DVDs and floppy disks. Dust and general grime accumulating over a period of time can also cause problems.

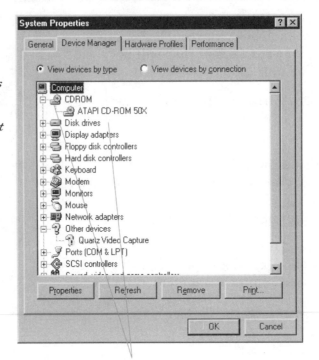

| Double click the drive's category to reveal the device's driver

Click the device, click *Properties* and make sure it hasn't been disabled in the *Disable in this hardware profile* box.

Then check it isn't in conflict with another device. If this is the case you will see a yellow exclamation mark over the icon in *Device Manager*. Resolve this by using the procedure detailed in the **Resource Conflict Troubleshooter**.

If it isn't listed then the device's driver hasn't been installed or is corrupt. Re-install it by using the *Add New Hardware* wizard in the *Control Panel*. If the device came with an installation CD or floppy, then have it to hand.

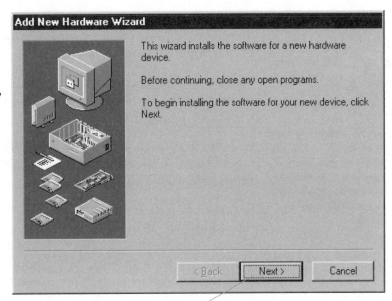

A good way of checking the power supply to a CD-ROM, DVD or floppy drive is to temporarily connect it to a different drive in the PC and see if that works. If it does then you know the power supply is OK.

| Click here to start the *Add New Hardware* wizard

If there is still no joy then you have a problem with the device itself or its connections. Firstly, make sure it has power. If the LED (light) works or you can hear activity then the power is present. You can also check the power by temporarily connecting it to a different device and seeing if that works.

CD-ROM and floppy drives are so cheap nowadays that it's hardly worth the bother of trying to repair them. Remember also that they are very simple to install.

If the device was working and then suddenly stopped, it is unlikely there will be a problem with the connections unless something has happened which could dislodge them. Nevertheless open up the system case and ensure all the plugs are firmly seated in their respective sockets.

The only other explanation is a defective drive unit. Fortunately, these devices, particularly floppy disk drives, are relatively inexpensive to replace. Installing them is also a simple and straightforward procedure which anyone can tackle. All you need is a suitable screwdriver.

CD Problems

CDs are prone to physical damage. Handle them with care and try to avoid scratching them. If a particular CD refuses to play properly, make sure it's clean and try to remove any scratches with a household abrasive such as brass or silver polish.

The drive appears to be working, indicated by lights and drive activity, but it isn't running your CDs or not running them properly.

The first thing to check is that you are not inserting the disk the wrong way round (yes, people do do it). The label should be facing up.

If the disk is dirty (fingerprints or dust) it might very well refuse to play. Clean the CD by using a proprietary cleaning agent and a soft lint free cloth.

Severely scratched CDs are quite likely to be ignored or misread by the drive. However, it is sometimes possible to restore disks in this condition depending on the severity of the damage. Basically, a CD is comprised of various layers with the top layer being a fine protective film of aluminium. Because the data tracks are under this layer it's usually possible to remove the scratches without damaging the data tracks. For this you will need a very fine household abrasive such as brass or silver polish. Using a soft cloth gently rub the surface of the disk until the scratches have been removed as far as possible.

If your CD-ROM drive works intermittently or is causing the PC to freeze or crash, then try cleaning the lens. The easiest way to do this is with a lens cleaning disk.

If you find that the CD-ROM drive appears to be working intermittently, i.e. some disks won't play at all while others take ages to load up or don't play properly, the problem will almost certainly be a dirty laser lens inside the drive. If this is the case you will also quite probably be experiencing crashes and freezes when loading certain disks.

The solution, not surprisingly, is to clean the lens. There are two ways to do this. You can either physically dismantle the drive unit to gain access to the lens or you can purchase a proprietary lens cleaning disk from a computer store. Of the two methods, the first will give better results, but is obviously much more of a performance. Try a cleaning disk first and if it doesn't have the desired effect, then do it the hard way.

DVD Problems

Not all graphics cards can handle the increased demand of DVD video. If you have added your DVD drive to an existing system rather than purchasing a system already containing a DVD drive, you must be sure your graphics card can handle it. At the very least, ensure you are running it with the latest driver.

You should also make sure that you have the latest version of DirectX installed.

DVD Playback is Slow or Jerky

While CDs and DVDs employ the same technology, there is a big difference between them. This lies in the amount of data they hold. A DVD can hold up to 18 GB of data in comparison to 650 MB on a CD.

It is this characteristic that makes DVDs perfect vehicles for full screen video. This same characteristic however, can cause problems when the DVD is played on a computer. Because of the tremendous amount of data involved, the PC must be up to the job in terms of CPU speed and graphics card capabilities. If it isn't then slow and jerky video will be the result. This problem is much more likely to occur in systems which have had a DVD player added to them rather than systems supplied with one. It may be necessary to upgrade the PC's CPU and graphics card in order to achieve satisfactory playback. At the very least, make sure there are no other applications running and that the latest graphics card driver has been installed.

Playing DVD video on your PC is very resource intensive. Keep other applications to the bare minimum. Also, turn off your screen saver when you play a movie. You won't be using your keyboard or mouse while you watch and your screensaver won't recognize the DVD as activity enough to keep itself from activating.

Dirty or scratched DVDs will react in exactly the same way as CDs. Playback will be slow, intermittent and with dropped frames. Keep the disks clean and remove any scratches by using a household abrasive such as brass or silver polish.

DVDs Won't Play

If a region code error is reported when playing back a DVD movie, you are trying to play a DVD that is for a different region.

Another problem with DVDs arises as a result of the paranoia of the film companies. In an effort to limit the potential loss of revenue caused by illegal copying, they have introduced a system of regional coding whereby DVDs marketed in one part of the world cannot be played in another. Verify that the regional coding of the DVD being played matches the regional coding of the DVD drive. The jewel case that the DVD comes in should document the region in which the DVD is meant to be played. If the DVD was acquired from an 'unofficial' source then this will almost certainly be the cause of the problem.

DVDs/CDs Don't Auto Play

When you place a disk in the drive it should run automatically. However not everybody wants this feature and so it can be disabled. Make sure this is not the case with yours.

Should you, for any reason, be unable to open the disk tray on your DVD or CD-ROM drive unit by pressing the 'open' button, there is another way to do it. Somewhere on the front of the unit you will see a tiny pin hole. By inserting a paperclip or something similar, you should be able to open the tray manually.

Go to *Control Panel, System, Device Manager* and click your DVD/CD-ROM drive. Click *Properties, Settings* and in *Options* make sure *Auto Insert Notification* has been ticked.

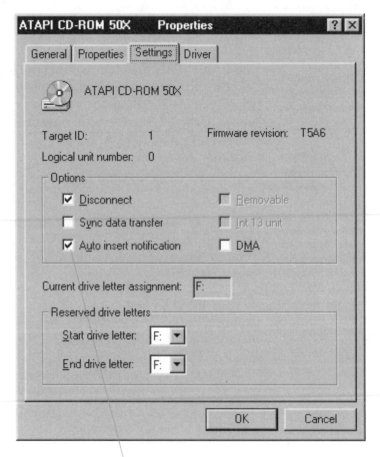

Tick *Auto insert notification* box

Floppy Disk Problems

If you find you can't save a file to a particular floppy disk, it could be a result of the disk not having been formatted. If this is the case the drive won't be able to write to it. You will get an error message to this effect.

Format the disk by right-clicking on the floppy drive icon in *My Computer* and then selecting *Format*. Now you will be able to use it.

Before any magnetic storage medium can be used it must first be formatted. This procedure organises the magnetic surface of the disk into neat sectors and tracks. These act like signposts and tell the read/write heads exactly where to read or write data. Formatting provides a way for Windows to organise and locate data saved to a disk.

It's very rare these days for floppy disks to be supplied in an unformatted condition. However should this be the case, select the Full Format option as this will also check the disk for physical damage.

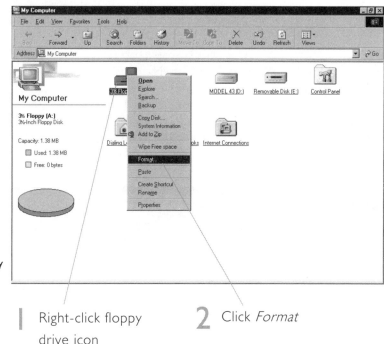

| Right-click floppy drive icon

2 Click *Format*

The same problem can be caused by *write protection*. When this happens you will get an error message as below.

Write protection provides a means of ensuring that valuable data cannot be accidentally altered or deleted from a floppy disk.

The solution is to remove the *write protection* by sliding the small black tab on the back of the disk to close the hole.

Yet another cause of being unable to save to a floppy disk is *compression*. If a disk has been *compressed*, it must first be *mounted* before it can be used. If this is the case the disk will contain a *Readthis* file which details the procedure.

Before any compressed disk can be accessed, it must first be mounted. This procedure makes the disk accessible to the computer's file system.

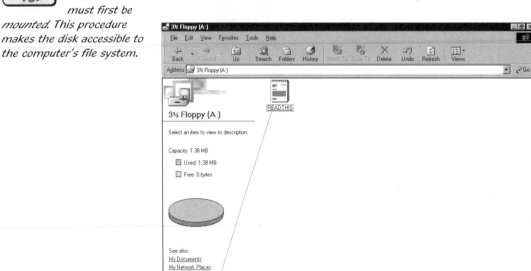

Open this file and you will see instructions on how to mount the disk

Memory Troubleshooter

Memory faults in computers can be among the more difficult to diagnose due to the range of problems that they can cause. This is further complicated by the fact that there are two types of memory – real and virtual. Real memory (Random Access Memory or RAM for short) is provided by the memory chips on your motherboard, while virtual memory is created by Windows to be used as and when required.

Hardware faults, i.e. with the memory chips themselves, are rare, a fact which holds true for computer hardware in general. However, when it does happen you will usually get an error message on the screen which can help in the diagnosis.

Faults on the software side of the memory system are much more common and obscure in their origins and are thus correspondingly more difficult to pin down.

Covers

Diagnosis | 70

Too Many Applications Running | 71

Virtual Memory | 72

Hard Disk Space | 73

Retained Memory | 74

Chapter Eight

Diagnosis

One way of establishing exactly what type of memory is in your computer, is to acquire a utility which will analyse your system and tell you exactly what's in it. These types of program are freely available for download over the Internet from sites such as www.winfiles.com. Some are completely free, others will only work for a certain length of time or a limited number of times.

Memory (RAM) capacity is one of the most important factors in overall system performance. It stands to reason therefore, that when system performance drops off, memory should be an automatic suspect.

In the same way that you'd immediately notice a sudden reduction in your car's acceleration, so it is with your PC. If for example, your programs suddenly start taking six seconds to open whereas before they took two, then the PC's performance has dropped off. This issue of poor or reduced performance is one of the most common problems with a system that has a memory problem. In nearly every case it comes down to not enough memory in the system (this doesn't necessarily mean the capacity of the memory chips).

Other symptoms include an unusual incidence of crashes and lockups. These can be general or specific to particular applications.

Error messages such as *This Program has Performed an Illegal Operation* and *Fatal Exception Error* can also usually be traced to lack of memory.

When handling computer hardware such as circuit boards and chips, it is essential to earth yourself first. If you don't, the static electricity in your body can cause permanent damage to these components.

Memory hardware faults usually manifest themselves during bootup, which is a good clue. Unfortunately this is often a refusal to complete the boot process. Also, they are almost always accompanied by an error message, which can be useful in determining what action to take next. However, the only way to be really sure of a particular RAM chip's integrity is to replace it with one known to be good.

The problem with replacing RAM chips however, is that of establishing exactly which one is in your system, as there are so many different types. Probably the easiest way is to phone the manufacturer of your PC and ask. Or you could unplug one of the chips and take it to a repair shop and ask them for a replacement. Having obtained the necessary chip, it's simply a question of replacing each chip in turn, rebooting each time until the faulty module has been identified.

The rest of this chapter examines the main reasons a PC might become low in memory and how to overcome them.

Too Many Applications Running

To see how many applications you have running at any one time, hit Ctrl+Alt+Del. This reveals the Close Program utility with which you can also shut down any programs that you don't need.

The amount of memory any computer system has physically available, corresponds to the capacity of the installed RAM chips. If any program (or combination of programs) needs more than this then they simply won't run, or if they do, will run extremely slowly. Typically you will see an error message as shown below.

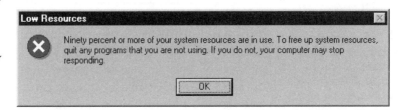

When you see this type of message take a look at the amount of System Resources (memory) you have available. Right-click *My Computer*, click *Properties* and *Performance*.

Random Access Memory (RAM) is one of the most crucial elements in a computer and lack of it can cause a whole range of seemingly inexplicable faults. Because these types of faults are so unspecific they are generally referred to as System Instability. When you get error messages such as Illegal Operations, you should immediately suspect your memory.

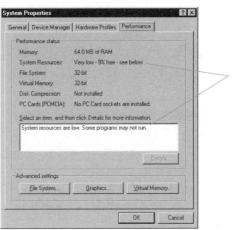

In this example the system is warning you that you are running low on memory

The odds are that you have too many programs running simultaneously. This problem can also occur when trying to run the latest resource hungry games on a low specified machine. The simple answer is to close some of the programs down. Either that or install more RAM.

To a certain degree however, Windows has an answer, which leads us to the next section – Virtual Memory.

Virtual Memory

When the operating system discovers it has less RAM available than it needs to run a particular application, it gets round the problem by 'borrowing' the required amount of memory from the hard disk and placing it in a specially created file called the Swap file. As the program is run the required data is swapped between this file and RAM as needed. In most cases this procedure works fine and the user is not even aware of what is going on. There is a drawback however and this lies in the fact that the hard disk operates a lot slower than RAM, the net result being that the program currently being accessed may run considerably slower than normal. You may also notice an unusual amount of hard disk activity – a phenomenon known as 'thrashing', which can produce wear and tear on the drive mechanism.

 It is possible for users to change the virtual memory settings which Windows sets by default. The advantage of doing this is that the PC's performance can be speeded up slightly. However, unless you know exactly what you are doing, you are more likely to actually make things worse.

There is a control which allows you to specify your own virtual memory settings. You can access this by right-clicking *My Computer* and selecting *Properties*. Then click on the *Performance* tab and then on the *Virtual Memory* button.

NOTE: This adjustment is for experienced users only and under normal circumstances there will be no need to fiddle with it. Let Windows handle virtual memory settings.

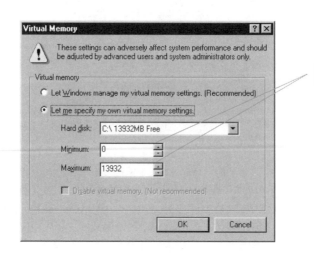

Use the drop down boxes to enter your own virtual memory settings

Hard Disk Space

As long as there is sufficient space on the hard drive, virtual memory usually works fine. If however the free space drops below a certain level, then things can slow to a snail's pace. You will almost certainly see a message stating that you don't have enough memory or resources available. (A good rule of thumb is to have a minimum of 10 per cent of the hard disk free.)

Memory problems aren't only caused by lack of RAM. If the available space on your hard drive is sufficiently low, then you can get problems with virtual memory which runs from the hard drive. To find out just how much space your drive has available click My Computer on the desktop and then right-click your hard drive's icon.

When this happens, the solution is to free up some space on the hard disk either by deleting stuff you don't need, compressing it or upgrading to a larger capacity drive.

Find out if this is the problem by clicking *My Computer*, right-clicking the hard drive icon and then selecting *Properties*. You will see a pie chart indicating how much disk space has been used and how much is currently available. If you are low on space click the *Disk Cleanup* button to free some up.

This book assumes readers have Windows set in single click mode. If you have it set in double click mode, in some cases you will need to double click where the text reads 'click'.

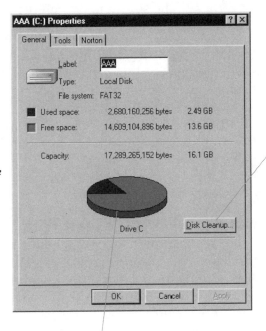

Use the *Disk Cleanup* utility if you are low on drive space

2 The pie chart indicates how much disk space you have available

Retained Memory

Too many fonts installed on your computer can use up resources and also slow down the bootup procedure. Only install fonts you really need. Click on the Fonts icon in the Control Panel to access a utility for deleting unnecessary fonts.

All programs when initially run, load their files into the systems RAM from where they are accessed by the CPU. When the program is closed down the program uninstalls these files, i.e. clears the RAM. That's the theory anyway. In practice however, spurious bits of data are often left behind and over time these can build up and uselessly occupy a large part of the memory. The longer this goes on the more likely it becomes that a particular program you run will be unable to find enough RAM to function properly. Alternatively, it will try to access a part of RAM which is already occupied. When this happens, the program will crash.

This problem usually occurs when a computer is run for a long time without being shut down. To understand why this is so, you need to be aware that a RAM chip will only retain the data it is holding as long as it's powered up. As soon as it loses its power source, it releases its data, i.e. it clears itself. This then is the solution. Switch the computer off then restart it. The RAM chips will now be empty.

One way of reducing the demand on your system memory, is to reduce the monitors colour depth setting. This can be done by right-clicking on the desktop, then selecting Properties, Settings.

Similarly, if during the running of a program, the PC is suddenly rebooted incorrectly (e.g., a crash), the program's files may well be retained by RAM as they haven't been given a chance to uninstall themselves. This could leave insufficient memory for subsequent programs. In this situation you are quite likely to get an error message stating that *The system is dangerously low on resources*. Again, the cure is to shut down and then restart the PC – this action will clear RAM.

Not Enough RAM to Start With

If you are planning to run the latest resource-hungry games or video editing programs, be sure you have enough RAM to cope with the enormous demand these applications will place on your system.

Some applications use a tremendous amount of system resources. Games are a typical example. Many of the ones now coming on the market require your PC to have a minimum of 64 MB of RAM. If you have less, you really are on a non-starter.

Display/Graphics Troubleshooter

Problems in this area can usually be attributed to either the monitor or the graphics card and/or their settings, although there can be other causes.

Image faults are usually fairly simple to isolate and rectify and can range from a faintly flickering display to one which is completely scrambled and unintelligible.

Covers

Flickering Display | 76

Incorrect Display | 77

Can't Change Resolution/Colour Depth | 78

Miscellaneous Image Faults | 80

Chapter Nine

Flickering Display

Display issues don't just relate to the monitor. They are also affected by the graphics card.
It's also worth remembering that the settings for one can affect the settings for the other.

There are basically two kinds of screen flicker you are likely to see on your monitor – one that's so fast it's just faintly perceptible and one that's similar to the flicker you occasionally see on your TV screen.

In the first case this is caused by having the refresh rate of your graphics card set too low. Right-click on an empty area of the desktop and select *Properties*. Then select the *Settings* tab and click on the *Advanced* button at the bottom. Click on the *Adapter* tab and you will see a *Refresh rate* setting at the bottom. Change it to a higher setting (75Hz at least) or Optimal and this should stop the flickering.

Electrical interference can come from many sources.
A noisy mains supply is one. Another possibility is the close proximity of motors or generators. Electrical storms, i.e. lightning, can cause severe interference. A faulty power supply unit on your PC can cause problems as well.

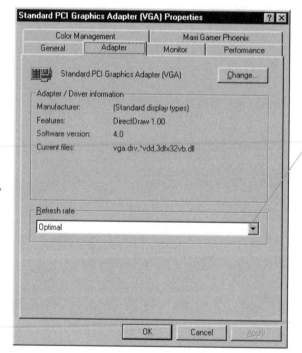

Set your *Refresh rate* here

In the second case the problem will be the same as on your TV, i.e. electrical interference. Move any item of electrical or electronic equipment away from the vicinity of the monitor. The problem could also be caused by the mains supply to the PC. Try installing a surge suppressor to iron out any voltage fluctuations.

Incorrect Display

Distorted Display

This means a display that is mis-shapen or deformed. The usual cause of this is an external magnetic source interfering with the electromagnets within the monitor. Unshielded speakers are a possible though unlikely cause, as modern day speakers are shielded for this precise reason.

The higher the refresh rate, the more stable your display will be. The higher your resolution, the sharper your display will be. Obviously you want the highest settings you can get for each. However, the higher they are set, the more likely it will be that either the monitor or the graphics card will be unable to support one or other of these settings. If this is the case you will end up with a scrambled display. Getting the balance right is basically a trade off and will be achieved by a process of trial and error.

Scrambled Display

If your monitor is completely scrambled, i.e. unintelligible, then either your refresh rate is too high or the monitor resolution is set higher than the graphics card can support at the refresh rate selected. Reboot the PC into *Safe Mode* and then lower the refresh rate. Restart the PC. If the display is still scrambled reboot into *Safe Mode* again, right-click on the desktop, click *Properties, Settings* and then lower the resolution by dragging the slider back. Reboot again and everything should now be OK.

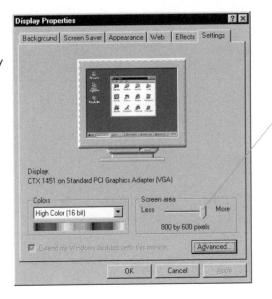

Adjust screen resolution by dragging the slider

Can't Change Resolution/Colour Depth

This is a common problem and is a result of the wrong graphics card driver having been installed.

Check to see if this is the case by right-clicking the desktop and then *Properties, Settings, Advanced*. Then click *Adapter*. The driver currently being used will be detailed.

Another way of establishing which graphics card driver is currently installed, is by looking in the Device Manager under Display Adapters.

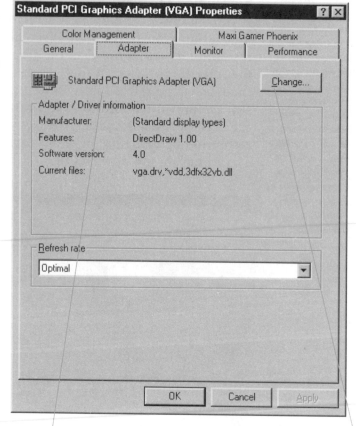

| Current graphics card driver

2 Click here if you want to install a different driver

If it is incorrect, insert the graphics card driver CD in the CD-ROM drive, click the *Change* button and then in the next dialog box, click *Automatic search for a better driver (Recommended)*.

If you are uncertain of what driver to install, let Windows do the work of finding and installing the one most suitable.

3 Click here and then click *Next*. Windows will go off and look for the driver

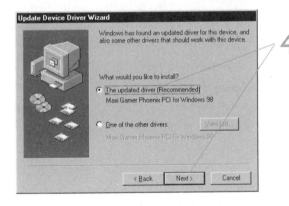

4 Windows tells you which driver it has found. If it is the correct one click *Next* and Windows will install it

You will find that you are now able to change your desktop resolution and colour depth.

Miscellaneous Image Faults

Display Blank

See the **Bootup Troubleshooter**.

Monitor Display is the Wrong Size

The general rule of thumb is that 14 inch monitors have a resolution of 640 X 480, 15 inch monitors have a resolution of 800 X 600 and 17 inch monitors have a resolution of 1024 X 768. This isn't set in stone but by and large these settings work best.

This is simply corrected by changing the screen resolution as already described. The higher the screen resolution, the smaller the displayed image will be. Which resolution is right for you depends on the size of your monitor.

Shadowing/Ghosting

This problem is usually caused by a faulty cable connecting the graphics card to the monitor. Also, using an extension cable, which may be too long, can cause the same problem. Another possibility is a poorly seated graphics card.

Poor Focus

If the displayed image is blurred you could be using a refresh rate which is too high. Try lowering it. This problem can also be caused by using an extension cable. Adjusting the Moiré control (see below) can help to improve the clarity of text.

Moiré Patterns

Moiré patterns are natural interference phenomena that appear in all colour CRT displays. These patterns appear as ripples or waves that are superimposed on the screen image. They are most noticeable on high resolution displays.

Advanced Power Management is a common cause of a seemingly dead monitor and can cause headaches to the uninitiated. It can cause problems in other areas as well and you are really well advised to disable it.

You can minimise or eliminate them by using your monitor's Moiré reduction control, slightly defocusing the image using the monitor's focus control, changing the image size or the screen resolution or by using a bright window background colour. The dimmer the colour, the more noticeable the Moiré patterns will be.

Sound Troubleshooter

To many people the sound aspect of their PC is of lesser importance than the graphics, since for many programs sound isn't needed at all. Typical examples are office applications such as word processors and spreadsheets. However for those who use their computers to play games and run multimedia applications, sound, while still not essential, is definitely part of the experience.

Furthermore most of us would miss all those little jingles and clicks that Windows likes to play. It just isn't the same without them.

So although the sound element in a PC isn't as crucial as other aspects, it's definitely worth having.

This chapter examines what's likely to go wrong and how to deal with it.

Covers

No Sound | 82

Sound Card | 84

General Sound Problems | 85

CD-ROM Drive has no Sound | 88

Chapter Ten

No Sound

The first thing to establish is whether the PC is producing any sounds at all anywhere on the system or merely from within certain applications.

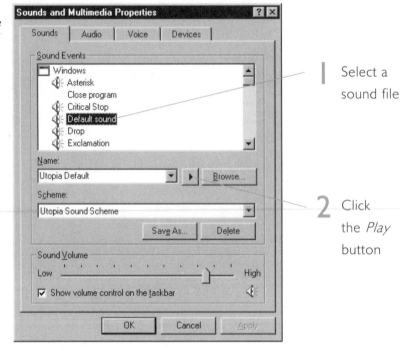

Some PCs come with the sound card built in to the motherboard.
With this type of setup the speakers are powered and will not work unless they are plugged into the mains supply. They will also need to be switched on.

Firstly, try playing a music CD on the CD-ROM drive. Secondly, try playing a WAV file by going to *Control Panel, Multimedia, Sounds*. From the *Events* window, select an item that has a speaker icon and then click the *Play* button.

1 Select a sound file

2 Click the *Play* button

Establish whether your sound card is compatible with the version of Windows you are running. Find out by visiting the Microsoft web site.

If either of these tests produces sound then your problem is not too serious as they indicate that the sound card, speakers and their connections are all OK. The problem will most likely be specific to a particular application. Re-installing it will usually fix the problem.

If you cannot get any WAV files to play and there's nothing from the CD-ROM drive, then you need to look further.

Make sure your speakers are connected to the correct socket on your sound card. This should be the Speaker Out socket.

Are the speakers connected to the right socket? They should be connected to the 'Speaker Out' socket. If they are powered speakers, are they switched on and is the volume turned up? Also, check the *Volume control* in Windows by clicking the speaker icon on the right hand side of the taskbar. If it isn't there then go to *Control Panel, Multimedia, Sounds*. At the bottom, you will see a volume slider control. Make sure it's turned up to at least half way. Click the *Show volume control on the taskbar* box.

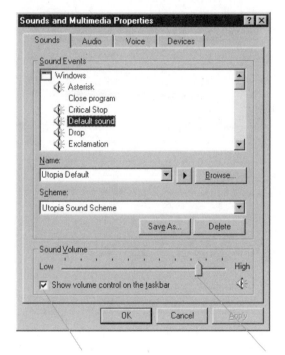

2 Tick here if you want the volume control to be displayed on the taskbar

| *Sound Volume* control

Sound Card

The next thing to check is that your sound card is correctly installed. Go to *Control Panel, Multimedia*.

On the *Audio* tab, you should see two areas: *Playback* and *Recording*. If these are greyed out and have *None* listed under *Preferred device*, then your sound card drivers have not been installed. If you do have a device listed here, such as 'AWE64 Wave Out' or 'Sound Blaster 16', then your drivers are installed. Make sure to check the *Show volume control on the taskbar* box.

Insufficient Random Access Memory (RAM) really hampers audio performance. For today's applications, you need at least 32MB of RAM. Sound applications place a heavy load on the Central Processing Unit (CPU). If you also have other programs running simultaneously, your sound performance may be adversely affected. Try closing them down.

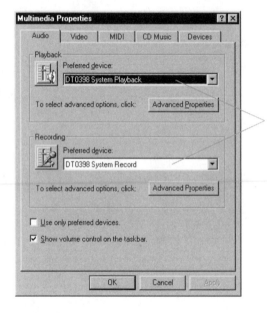

These two boxes indicate the sound card is installed

If the sound card driver is not installed then click the *Add New Hardware* wizard in the *Control Panel* and follow the instructions.

Next check the sound card for resource conflicts. See the **Resource Conflict Troubleshooter** for instructions on how to do this.

Finally check that the card is located properly in its socket.

General Sound Problems

Jerky or Intermittent Sound

In nearly all cases, intermittent or jerky sound is caused by a lack of system resources (low memory) although the problem can also be caused by faulty speakers, cables or cable connections. Check the amount of RAM available by right-clicking *My Computer* and selecting *Properties, Performance*. If your resources are low, then free some up by quitting any running programs.

Another reason can be if your sound card is digital but the speakers are analogue. Select Sounds and Multimedia Properties from the Control Panel, click on the Audio tab, then the Volume button for Sound Playback, ensure Advanced Controls is selected from the Options menu, to display the Advanced button, which when clicked should show a check box for Digital Output Only – uncheck this to make the sound card and speakers compatible in analogue.

Percentage of available system resources

If you're using USB speakers, unplug all other USB peripherals, including any USB hubs, and make sure the speakers are directly plugged into one of the PC's USB ports. This eliminates any possible bandwidth drain on the USB channel that other devices may be causing.

Crackling or Noisy Sound

The cause of this irritating problem is electromagnetic interference and to solve it you must locate the source of the interference and remove it. Try removing your sound card from its existing socket and moving it to a new one as far away as possible from the other cards.

Electromagnetic interference can result in crackling or noisy sound.

Sources can be both external and internal.

Another thing to try is to remove any electrical equipment from the vicinity of your speakers.

Also ensure your speakers and speaker cables are shielded against magnetic interference.

Problems with Specific Sound Files

If a specific sound refuses to play but others do then it is certainly either missing or corrupted. Check by opening *Multimedia* in the *Control Panel*, click any file in the *Sound Events* window and then click *Browse*. This opens the *Media* folder, which contains all your sound files.

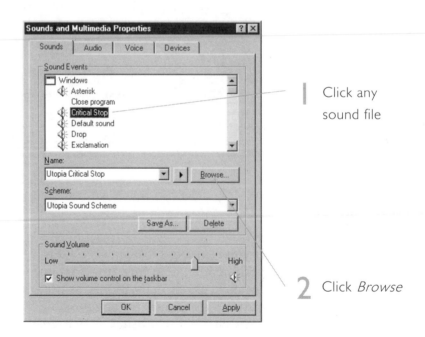

1 Click any sound file

2 Click *Browse*

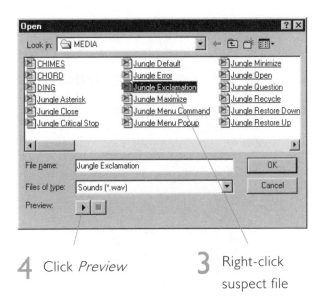

4 Click *Preview*

3 Right-click
suspect file

Find the suspect file, right-click it and then click *Preview*. If the file is OK, it will play. If not, it is corrupted and must be re-installed.

Distorted Sound

Never have your speakers turned up too high. This will result in distorted output. Lower the volume setting to a level which they can support.

The usual cause of this problem is having the volume set at a level which the speakers can't support. This happens particularly with cheaper speakers. The solution is to simply lower the volume to a level which the speakers can handle comfortably.

Also, try the following: Go to *Control Panel, Multimedia, Audio*. Click *Advanced Properties*. Click *Performance*. Click *Restore Defaults*. Now move the *Acceleration* slider to the left. This may solve the problem.

This fault can also be caused by a resource conflict involving the sound card. Check this possibility out in *Device Manager*. See Chapter Eleven.

CD-ROM Drive has no Sound

Go to *Control Panel, System, Device Manager*. Click the CD-ROM driver. Click the *Settings* tab.

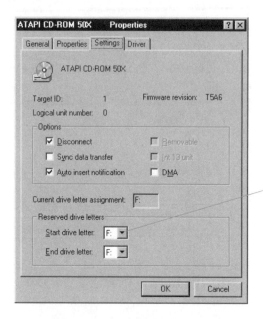

Make sure the CD-ROM drive is set to the appropriate drive letter. This is usually 'D' but if you have several drives it could be a different letter as shown here

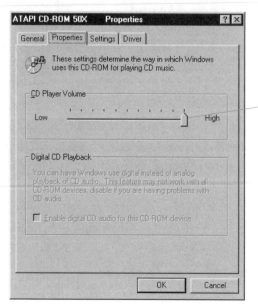

2 Then click the *Properties* tab and make sure the *CD Player Volume* is set to *High* by dragging the slider if necessary

Resource Conflict Troubleshooter

A resource conflict is probably one of the most likely faults to be encountered on a PC. Their effects are usually specific to a particular hardware device, which isn't too serious if it's a sound card for example. However it might be your hard drive, in which case you could have serious problems.

This chapter explains just what resource conflicts are, how to identify them and how to resolve them.

Covers

What is a Resource Conflict? | 90

Device Manager | 91

Identifying Resource Conflicts | 92

Resolving Resource Conflicts | 93

Device Manager Error Codes | 97

Chapter Eleven

What is a Resource Conflict?

First we need to understand just what is meant by the term computer resource.

A computer's resources are:

Resource conflicts almost always occur as a result of installing a new item of hardware or software. Sound cards and SCSI adapters are by far the most likely culprits as they use an enormous amount of system resources.

- The Interrupt Request Channels (IRQ)

- The Direct Memory Access Channels (DMA)

- The Input/Output Port Addresses (I/O)

The purpose of these resources is as follows:

- IRQs allow the systems hardware devices to communicate with the CPU in an orderly fashion.

- DMAs allow data transfer directly to RAM by bypassing the CPU. These channels are used by high-speed communications devices such as sound cards and SCSI adapters.

- I/Os are used by device drivers to communicate with software applications.

The most likely resource to cause problems is IRQs because there's usually not enough of them to meet the demand.

Controlling everything, we have the operating system (Windows in most cases). It's the role of Windows to allocate the available system resources to wherever they are needed. By and large it all works extremely well but every once in a while, Windows loses control of things. When it does individual devices begin competing against each other, claiming the same resources as their own. Thus we have resource *conflicts*.

Classic signs of resource conflict are:

- System fails to boot

- System freezes during boot

- Erratic device behaviour

Device Manager

Windows *Device Manager* is one of the most important troubleshooting tools on your PC. Proper use of this utility will allow you to identify and repair the resource conflicts, which are an inevitable part of running a computer. The utility can be accessed by going to *Control Panel, System* and clicking the *Device Manager* tab.

Click *System*

The Device Manager is Windows diagnostic and troubleshooting aid for sorting out resource conflicts. This tool is located in the Control Panel under System.

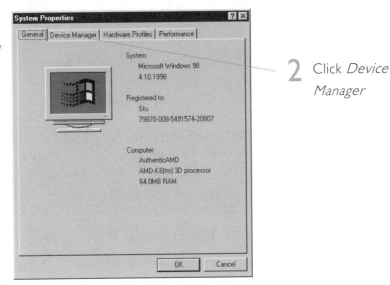

2 Click *Device Manager*

Identifying Resource Conflicts

Before any resource conflict can be repaired, it must first be identified as such. Click on *Device Manager* and you will see listed various categories for all the hardware devices in your system. Double clicking on a category, or clicking the + symbol next to it, will reveal the specific device within it. If any of the devices are flagged with a yellow exclamation mark, you know immediately that it is conflicting with another device or cannot find any free resources. A red 'X' symbol indicates the device has been disabled.

The Device Manager uses coloured symbols to identify devices that have a problem. Each symbol indicates a different type of problem.

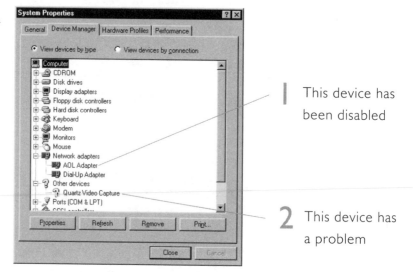

| This device has been disabled

2 This device has a problem

Click the offending device and then click *Properties* at the bottom. This will take you to the *General* tab and under *Device Status* you will see a status message telling you what the situation is. There are in fact about 30 different messages, some of the more common ones being:

- This Device Is Working Properly

- This Device Is Causing A Resource Conflict

- The Drivers For This Device Are Not Installed

- This Device Is Disabled

Resolving Resource Conflicts

Physically removing devices from a PC is a good way of eliminating them as a cause of a particular problem. However many people will be wary of doing this as it's all too easy to forget what cables went where, etc. Device Manager offers a much easier and safer way to do this. Click the device in question and then click Properties. Under Device usage click the Disable in this hardware profile check box. The device will then be effectively removed from the system.

Having established which device is causing the problem, you basically have two ways to go. The first is the easiest but doesn't guarantee success.

In theory, any device added to a system should be automatically detected by Windows and assigned available resources.

This is the first option, i.e. let Windows remove the device from the system and then re-install it correctly.

Do it as follows: Click the offending device in *Device Manager* and then click on *Remove*. Windows will remove the item (i.e. uninstall it) and then prompt you to reboot. Do so and with a bit of luck, on restart Windows will find the hardware, install it correctly and assign the appropriate resources. If the device has an installation disk, have it to hand.

When we talk about a particular hardware device being installed, what we are really talking about is its driver. This is a small software program written specifically for the device which acts as an interface between the device and Windows.

1 Click the suspect device

2 Click the *Remove* button

If, however, Windows is unable to sort out the problem and sometimes it can't, then you'll have do it the hard way – manually. As an example, let's say we have a problem with Com Port 2. Go to *Device Manager*, click the offending device and click *Properties*.

There are two ways to resolve a resource conflict. The first is to let Windows do it automatically. This is also the easiest way. Unfortunately Windows doesn't always get it right. When this happens the problem will have to be sorted out manually.

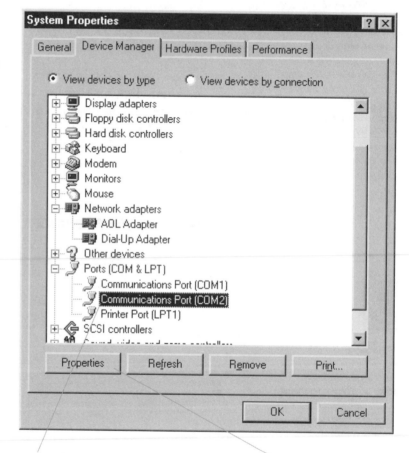

1 Click the device   2 Click *Properties*

In the next panel click *Resources*.

In the following screenshot we can see that COM Port 2 is trying to use the same IRQ as the Printer Port.

In order to resolve the conflict, we need to manually assign a new IRQ to COM Port 2.

 You should always leave the Use automatic settings check box ticked. This allows Windows to change the settings if and when it should prove necessary. If you leave it unticked, then the settings chosen are fixed. This may cause problems when other devices are installed.

3 Click the conflicting IRQ

4 Clear the *Use automatic settings* box

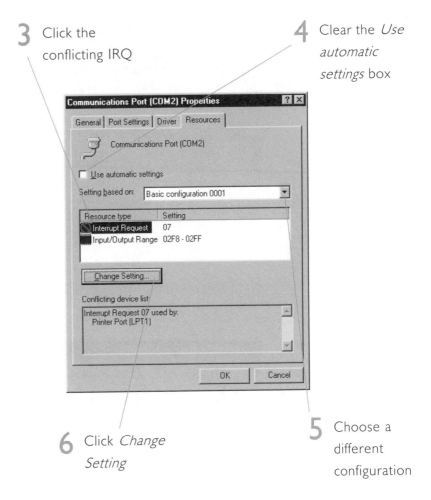

6 Click *Change Setting*

5 Choose a different configuration

You will now see the *Edit Interrupt Request* dialog box.

Windows tells you if the resource you have selected is appropriate in the Conflict information box. If the chosen resource conflicts with another device Windows will tell you which device this is.

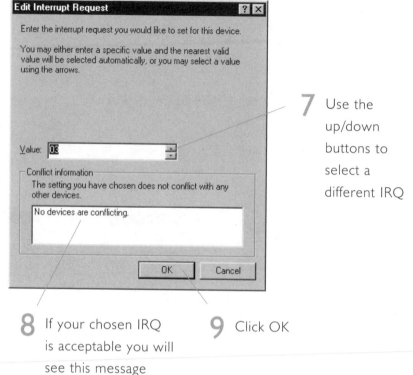

7 Use the up/down buttons to select a different IRQ

8 If your chosen IRQ is acceptable you will see this message

9 Click OK

NOTE: You may find that Windows won't allow you to change the settings.

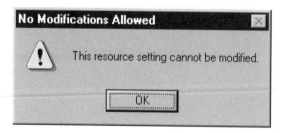

In this case try using a different *Basic Configuration* and if this doesn't work repeat the entire procedure with the other conflicting device.

Device Manager Error Codes

Device Manager error codes tell you what the problem is and what steps you can take to resolve it. This usually entails uninstalling the device causing the problem and then re-installing it.

The following is a list of the more common error codes:

Code 1 – This code means the system has not had a chance to configure the device. To resolve the problem, follow the instructions in the *Device Status* box. In addition, you may be able to resolve this issue by removing the device in *Device Manager*, and then running the *Add New Hardware* wizard from *Control Panel*.

Code 2 – The device driver has not been installed. Try removing the device from *Device Manager* and then running the *Add New Hardware* wizard from *Control Panel*.

Code 3 – The driver for this device is faulty. Either update the driver or use *Device Manager* to remove the device and then run the *Add New Hardware* wizard in *Control Panel*.

Code 6 – This code means there is a conflict between this device and another device. Resolve as described in this troubleshooter.

Code 7 – No configuration can be set for the device. If the device works correctly, you do not need to perform any steps to correct the code. If the device does not work correctly, use *Device Manager* to remove the device and then run the *Add New Hardware* wizard in *Control Panel*. If you continue to receive this error code and the device does not function properly, obtain an updated driver.

Code 8 – The device driver could not be found. In most cases, the solution is to re-install or update the driver.

Code 9 – The information in the registry for this device is invalid. It may be possible to resolve this error by using *Device Manager* to remove the device and then running the *Add New Hardware* wizard in *Control Panel*. If you continue to receive this error code, contact the hardware's manufacturer for the proper registry settings.

Code 11 – The device failed. Use *Device Manager* to remove the device and then run the *Add New Hardware* wizard in *Control Panel*. If the problem persists, contact the hardware manufacturer for updated drivers.

Code 13 – This code means the device failed due to a problem in the device driver. Use *Device Manager* to remove the device and then run the *Add New Hardware* wizard in *Control Panel*.

Code 14 – The device has a problem that may be resolved by restarting your computer.

Code 15 – The device's resources are conflicting with another device's resources. Carry out the steps described in this troubleshooter.

Code 16 – The device was not fully detected. When a device is not fully detected, all of its resources may not be recorded. To resolve this error code, click the *Resources* tab in the device's *Properties* to manually enter the settings.

Code 18 – This means that an error has occurred and the device needs to be re-installed. Do this by removing the device in *Device Manager* and then running the *Add New Hardware* wizard in *Control Panel*.

Code 19 – The registry returned an unknown result. Remove the device from *Device Manager*, and then re-detect it using the *Add New Hardware* wizard in *Control Panel*.

Code 21 – The device has a problem that may be resolved by restarting your computer.

Code 22 – The device is disabled. Enable it as described in this troubleshooter. If the problem persists try re-detecting it using the *Add New Hardware* wizard.

Code 26 – This code means a device did not load. There may be a problem in the device driver or not all the drivers were installed. Use *Device Manager* to remove the device and then run the *Add New Hardware* wizard in *Control Panel*. If there is still no joy then try an updated driver.

Code 28 – The device was not installed completely. Try removing the device from *Device Manager* and using the *Add New Hardware* wizard to re-detect it. You may need to obtain updated drivers if the error still occurs.

System Instability Troubleshooter

Computers are predictable and reliable machines, they do exactly what they are told and nothing more or less. There is no other way for them to be as they can react only to the instructions they are given. As long as the instructions are logical and do not conflict and the operating conditions are within the designated parameters, the computer will perform exactly as it should.

However, tell it to do something which is impossible or doesn't make sense, i.e. is illogical, or subject it to something it isn't designed to cope with – extreme heat for example, and all of a sudden that reliability disappears out the window. The computer doesn't know how to react – things are happening inside it that shouldn't be. In short, it has become unstable.

Covers

Strategy | 100

Dealing with a Frozen or Hung PC | 101

Causes of System Instability | 102

Common Instability Error Messages | 106

Chapter Twelve

Strategy

Lockup or freeze describes a system that has suddenly become completely inactive whilst running. There are no error messages on the screen, the mouse pointer does not move, and pressing keys has no effect whatsoever.

Instability problems in a computer can be difficult to pin down, as there are so many possible causes. Both software and hardware can be to blame, not to mention external sources such as heat and electrical interference. Even worse, they can be intermittent, making it difficult to know whether a particular troubleshooting step has worked or not. Get as many clues as you can. Things to take note of include:

- Is the problem hardware or software related?

- Does the fault occur at random or can you reproduce it?

- What applications were running at the time?

- Does the problem occur when running a particular program or hardware device?

- Any changes to your computer immediately prior to the problem appearing

- Error messages

Having established as much as you can, the first thing to do is to try and work out if the fault is software or hardware related. Do this by starting up Windows in *Safe Mode* and see if it still occurs. If it doesn't then it is likely that your problem is software related. If, on the other hand, the error does still occur, there is probably something wrong with your hardware. This immediately cuts down the list of causes, thus eliminating many faultfinding procedures you might otherwise have to go through.

Typical indications of system instability are:

- Crashes, lockups/freezes, hanging

- Unpredictable behaviour

- Error messages such as *General Protection Faults*

Dealing with a Frozen or Hung PC

If your computer stops responding, the first thing to do is hit Ctrl+Alt+Del. This will open the Close Program dialog box which should reveal which application is causing the problem.

When presented with a frozen or hung PC, many people will immediately hit the reset button, which will certainly unfreeze the PC. Doing this however, can also lead to further problems. The first thing to be aware of is that Windows might have simply encountered a problem somewhere and is taking a little time in sorting it out. This isn't unusual. Be patient and wait for a few moments. Then, if nothing has happened, hit *Ctrl+Alt+Del* simultaneously which will bring up the *Close Program* dialog box.

In this box will be listed all the programs currently running and one of them should be indicated as *Not Responding*. Click this program and then click *End Task*. This should forcibly close the program and return you to Windows. Sometimes however, the computer will still fail to respond and it's at this point that you will have to resort to the reset button. Make sure on restarting that you run *ScanDisk* to repair any problems that this may have caused.

Hanging describes a less severe form of freezing. Things have ground to a halt, there are no error messages, but the machine is not completely dead. The mouse pointer may still move and pressing the Ctrl+Alt+Del key combination produces a response.

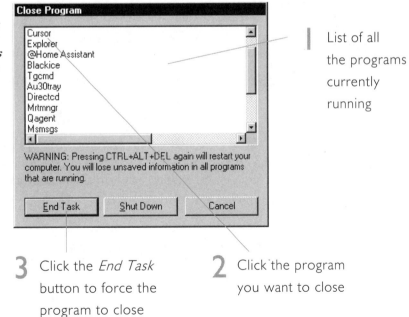

List of all the programs currently running

3 Click the *End Task* button to force the program to close

2 Click the program you want to close

Causes of System Instability

Incorrect Shutting Down

A typical example is having a memory intensive application such as a spreadsheet running when the PC suddenly crashes. It's quite possible that the application will not release all of the memory it was using, leaving the system short of memory on restart. Shutting the computer down properly will usually resolve this type of problem.

Damaged Hard Disk Drives

A crash is a somewhat unspecific piece of terminology but basically applies to a program or application that was working and then suddenly decided to stop working. This may take the form of causing the PC to abruptly reboot, return ing you unprompted to the Windows desktop or presenting you with a blue screen containing an error message such as Fatal Exception Error.

Hard disks can develop bad sectors over time, which can cause crashes. This problem can be corrected by running *ScanDisk*.

RAM Fragmentation

Fragmented memory is caused by programs which leave fragments of themselves in RAM when the program is closed down. Over a period these fragments accumulate and become scattered randomly in the RAM. This can have two effects.

Firstly, much of your systems RAM becomes unusable and this is when you are likely to see the *Your System Is Dangerously Low On Resources* error message.

Secondly, because the system is having to hunt around RAM for the data it wants, it slows everything down and this can have all sorts of effects, including crashes and lockups.

However, RAM fragmentation is only likely to happen if you run and use your PC over a long period without shutting it down. As soon as you do close it down, the memory clears itself.

Viruses

Viruses are a likely cause of general system instability and this possibility should be checked by running a virus program. Something that many people are not aware of is that very often the virus program itself can be causing instability. These programs use a lot of your systems resources.

Running Too Many Applications

The systems memory is where all of a particular program's files are loaded when that program is run. If too many programs are being run at the same time then it's possible that the system might not have enough memory to cope with them all. When this happens, crashes and lockups are a common result, as the various applications all compete for the available resources.

One way of finding out exactly what programs are currently active is to press *Ctrl+Alt+Del*. This brings up the *Close Program* dialog box which shows you every program or application that's running. Another way is to simply look at the icons in the middle of the taskbar. Each one of these icons represents an open program.

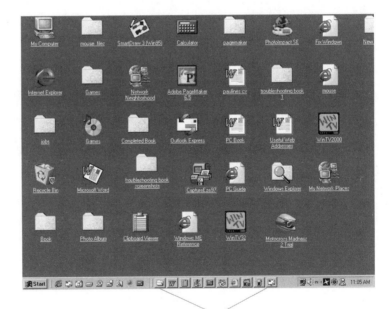

These icons show you which applications are running

The answer to the problem is quite simple – only run as many programs as your computer can handle.

Startup Programs

Programs and applications that run automatically when you start up Windows can be the cause of problems. Try disabling them and if the problem disappears then re-enable them, one by one, until the problem re-occurs. Then you'll know which program is to blame.

Conflicts

A good way of eliminating individual hardware devices as a potential cause of problems is by using the Device Manager. This allows you to disable any device by ticking the Disable in this hardware profile box.

A problem with a hardware device or its setup could be making your system jittery. Check this possibility by using the *Device Manager* in *Control Panel* to individually disable your system hardware.

Resource conflicts are a common cause of instability. This type of problem is usually caused when two items of hardware are allocated the same system resources. You will find that this often occurs when a new hardware device is installed and it conflicts with an existing device. See Chapter Eleven for instructions on how to check this out.

Clutter

Over a period of time (say a year), any PC which has been subjected to continuous use, will eventually become literally clogged up with spurious and redundant data. The unfortunate consequence of this is an almost imperceptible slowing down of the system and eventually possible general instability within that system.

Normal everyday use will often result in a PC eventually becoming unstable due to an inevitable buildup of redundant data. The only way to overcome this is to periodically do a clean installation of Windows. This will 'spring clean' your system and have it running like new again.

There is only one solution to this problem and that is to uninstall Windows and then re-install it. After you have done this, you will find that your computer runs like new and all manner of niggling little faults will have disappeared.

This course of action however, is not to be taken lightly and if it's not done correctly you will end up with a rather ugly and expensive paperweight on your desk.

Screensavers

Screensavers are really a legacy of the days when monitor screens could literally have an impression burnt in them by prolonged exposure to a static picture. Modern monitors do not suffer from this problem and so screensavers are really not needed at all nowadays. This is just as well as they are notorious for crashing PCs. Disable them by right-clicking the desktop, then clicking *Properties, Screensaver*. In the *Screensaver* drop down list, select *None*.

Never allow your computer to overheat. The effects of overheating can range from the irritating to the disastrous. System instability is one certain result.

Heat

Heat, or rather excessive heat, is the arch enemy of any computer system. Computer components are designed to withstand a certain amount of heat but if those tolerances are exceeded then frequent crashes and lockups are one certain result. Check to see the case fan is working and the air inlet at the back of the case is not obstructed. Acquire a can of compressed air at a computer shop and blow away the layer of dust that you will find on all the circuit boards. Dust is an insulator and too much of it will cause the boards to overheat.

Never remove dust from a circuit board by using a brush. Doing this will create static electricity which could well damage components on the board. Use a can of compressed air which is available from any computer shop.

Power Supplies

If, after checking all of the above, you still have an unstable system then about the only thing left is a faulty power supply. This need not necessarily be the computer's power supply – it could be the mains supply causing surges or voltage spikes. Computers don't like them. Eliminate this possibility by investing in a power surge suppressor.

If even this doesn't work then replace the PC's internal power supply unit. It's very easy to do and relatively inexpensive. Expect to pay around £30 for a power supply unit.

Common Instability Error Messages

There are far too many messages to be able to list them all, so we will concentrate on the ones more likely to crop up. It must be pointed out that the vast majority of instability problems are temporary in nature, and can be resolved by the simple expedient of switching off and then on again. These messages are also known as *Run Time Error Messages*.

General Protection Faults

One of the most common results of a General Protection Fault is the sudden loss of the work you were doing. This might only be five minutes work, which isn't too serious. On the other hand it might be a day's work or more. If it hasn't happened to you yet, it will eventually. Get into the habit of saving your work at regular intervals.

A General Protection Fault occurs when a program tries to access a part of the system memory (RAM) which is already in use. One of Windows' main purposes as an operating system is to provide memory to an application that is requesting it. If the memory it allocates is already in use by another program, General Protection Fault messages will be the result. Windows will then close down the program. The error itself will not cause any harm. The problem is that Windows forces you out of your program, so anything not previously saved is lost.

So what can you do when you get this type of fault? The first thing is to ensure you have enough hard drive space and RAM. Lack of memory is the most common cause of General Protection Faults. Next, run a defragmenting utility on your hard drive. Disable any screensavers you may have running. These are notorious for causing crashes, which is what a General Protection Fault basically is. Close any programs which may be running in the background. Reduce your desktop colour depth. For example, if it is currently set to 32 Bits, try lowering it to 16 Bits or 256 colours. The lower the colour depth, the less the resources being used. Do this by right-clicking on your desktop, click *Properties* and then *Settings*.

Fatal Exception Errors

These are very similar to General Protection Faults in that they can be caused by two applications trying to access the same section of RAM simultaneously. Hardware device drivers are common villains in this respect. They can also be caused by a fault in your system memory, i.e. a defective RAM module. Faulty CPUs can also give Fatal Exception Errors. These messages are usually displayed on a blue screen, the so called 'Blue Screen of Death'.

If you are being plagued by repeated Fatal Exception Errors, the first thing to do is use Safe Mode to determine whether the problem is hardware or software related. Remember, if the fault still occurs whilst the computer is running in Safe Mode, it will be hardware related.

To resolve persistent Fatal Exceptions you must first use *Safe Mode* (see page 27). This will establish if the cause of the problem lies in your software or hardware. If it is software related (indicated by the problem going away in *Safe Mode*), then the culprit is quite likely to be the program you were running when the error occurred. Try re-installing it. Then check out your device drivers in *Device Manager*. If however, the problem is still present in *Safe Mode*, then it will be something to do with your hardware. The most likely cause will be a faulty RAM chip. You could also have a failing or overheated CPU. Ensure it is being well cooled.

Invalid Page Faults

Invalid Page Fault errors happen when Windows runs out of RAM and attempts to use *Virtual Memory* but is unable to do so for some reason. When this occurs Windows throws up an Invalid Page Fault.

Do the following: Optimise your hard drive by running *ScanDisk* in its *Thorough* option to check for damaged sectors. Restore your registry by running SCANREG/ RESTORE as described on page 30. Then check your RAM by individually replacing the chip modules with one known to be good. As a last resort do a clean installation of Windows – see page 48.

Illegal Operations

These are probably the most common error messages of all and are usually specific to a particular application. For this reason they are also the easiest to resolve. In the vast majority of cases, simply uninstalling and then re-installing the program running when the error occurred will fix the problem.

Windows Protection Errors

This error is usually a result of an essential device driver not loading properly when Windows boots up. These errors are most likely to occur when a hardware device has been installed or changes made to the system.

Firstly, go into *Safe Mode* and uninstall any devices that may have just been installed. Reboot and if the problem has now cleared, try re-installing the device. Next, go into *Device Manager* and check for resource conflicts – see page 92. Run a virus checker on your system. Viruses can sometimes cause these errors, especially if the Windows system files are infected. Check your registry for corruption by running SCANREG. You may have a faulty RAM chip. Check these by replacing them one by one with a good RAM module. Do a clean installation of Windows – see page 48.

If none of these steps solves the problem, then you almost certainly have a problem with your motherboard.

Insufficient Memory Errors (or similar)

These types of error message imply that you don't have enough RAM to run an application. Don't be misled by this. What they really mean is that you are low on resources. This situation is caused when a program is shut down but fails to release all the memory it was occupying. The solution is simple. Shut down the PC and then reboot. This action will clear the memory.

Printing Troubleshooter

Printers are a well nigh essential part of a computer system as they allow the user to convert his or her digital data to something more permanent, i.e. hard copy.

Unfortunately, printing problems are very common and so this troubleshooter details the faults you are more likely to come across.

Also, remember that as Inkjets are far and away the most popular printers in the home environment, this is the type of printer covered in this chapter.

Covers

Printer Doesn't Print | 110

Files Print Slowly | 112

Poor Print Quality | 113

Software Settings | 114

Chapter Thirteen

Printer Doesn't Print

All printers use a special port designated specifically for them called LPT1. If this port is not selected the printer won't work. Check by going to Control Panel, Printers. Right-click your Printer icon, click Properties and under Details you will see the port to which your printer has been assigned. If it isn't LPT1, then select it from the drop down list and then click OK.

When troubleshooting printing problems, the first thing to establish is whether the printer itself has failed. Do this by seeing if it prints the test page as detailed in your printer documentation.

There are quite a few things which can prevent a printer from working, most of which are fairly straightforward to put right. When faced with this dilemma, absolutely the first thing to do is to ascertain whether the problem is a physical fault with the printer itself.

All modern printers have the facility to print a test page, which is done with the printer isolated from the computer. Typically, this involves disconnecting the printer interface cable and then pressing a combination of buttons. The procedure varies from printer to printer. If this test is successful it proves that the printer itself is OK and that the fault is software related or possibly with the connections. For instructions on how to carry out a printer test, refer to the instructions in your printer documentation.

If the printer doesn't print the test page then you have a problem with the printer itself. Before rushing it off to the repair shop though, check the obvious. Is the ink cartridge empty? Most printer software will indicate the level of ink remaining but this is by no means to be relied upon. A physical check is more reliable, i.e. take the cartridge out and have a close look at it. Also, run the nozzle cleaning utility in case the print nozzles are clogged up.

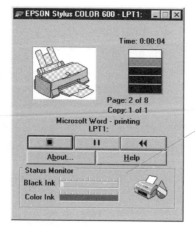

The *Status Monitor* tells you how much ink you have available in your cartridges (approx)

Assuming the test page does print as it should, then the next thing to check is that the printer cables are OK and connected to the correct ports. It is unlikely that there will be anything wrong with the printer interface cable but do check that the connections to both the printer and the PC are sound.

Having your printer connected to the system via another device such as a scanner or Zip drive can be a less-than-ideal arrangement as any problems with these devices could prevent the printer from receiving data from the PC.

A potential cause of problems is when you have your printer connected to the computer via another device such as a scanner or Zip drive. Any problems with the device in question could prevent the printer receiving data from the PC. Eliminate this possibility by connecting the printer directly to the computer.

Having eliminated the printer and its connections, you now know the problem is software related. The first thing to check is that you haven't simply *Paused* the printer. Do this by going to *Control Panel, Printers.* Click your printer and then in the *Printer* menu ensure that *Pause Printing* isn't checked.

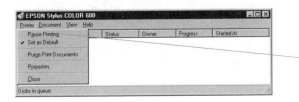

Make sure that *Pause Printing* hasn't been ticked

Problems can be caused by the program you are printing from. If you suspect this to be the case, try printing from a different program.

Establish that the fault isn't being caused by the program which you are printing from – your word processor for example. Do this by trying a different program such as *Wordpad* or *Notepad*. Open up one of these, type a few lines and then see if it prints. If it does then the program you were using originally is faulty and needs to be re-installed.

The printer's driver may have become corrupted. Check in *Control Panel, Device Manager, Ports (COM & LPT), Printer Port (LPT1).* If necessary re-install it. Also make sure the printer's resources are not conflicting with those of another device.

Files Print Slowly

If you are trying to print a large image file, it's possible that you don't have enough RAM to handle the amount of data, particularly if you also have other programs running. This can result in the file being printed very slowly or even not being printed at all.

Try reducing the resolution or colour depth of the file. Alternatively you could convert the file to a different format such as JPEG. This can reduce the size of the file considerably.

You can do all this in a Windows image editing program called *Imaging*. Go to *Start, Programs, Accessories* and then click *Imaging*.

If you find that documents are printing slower than you expected or want, then try lowering the dpi setting. The higher you have this set, the slower the print speed.

The same applies when printing out graphics. Also remember that the higher the resolution of the image file the slower it will print. In general resolutions higher than 300 dpi are unnecessary.

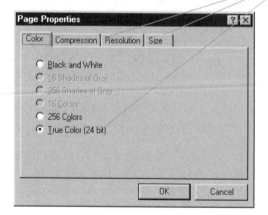

1 Open your image file, go to the *Page* menu and click *Properties*

2 Lower the size, colour depth and resolution of the image file by altering these settings

3 Click *Save as* on the *File* menu and choose a suitable low size image format such as *JPEG* before clicking *Save*

Poor Print Quality

The usual culprits here are the print nozzles which can clog up very easily. Given the fact that they are narrower than the thickness of a human hair, it's easy to understand why this often happens.

Refrain from using the nozzle cleaning utility any more than is absolutely necessary. This process uses up a lot of ink and given the price of ink cartridges, can be an expensive pastime.

Symptoms include gaps or faint areas in the printed document or image, poor quality colour output and white horizontal lines. Running the nozzle cleaning utility in your printer software should solve the problem. You may find though that you need to run it several times.

Try to use this utility sparingly as the head cleaning process involves shooting jets of ink through the nozzles to clear them. This procedure uses a surprising amount of ink. It can also cause the printer's platen to become contaminated with ink which will then be transferred to the document in the form of streaks and smudges. Cleaning the platen occasionally with a mild detergent will eliminate this.

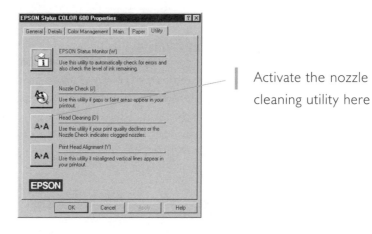

Activate the nozzle cleaning utility here

Keep your printer clean, especially the platen. Any deposits on it will be transferred to the document being printed.

Keep Your Printer Clean

Allowing your printer to get dirty is guaranteed to eventually adversely affect the quality of your printed documents. Although this doesn't affect the print quality as such, it can detract from the finished document in the form of smudges and streaks. Use a brush or a can of compressed air to clear away general dust and dirt from the inner workings of the printer.

Software Settings

Another cause of low quality printing is the selection of unsuitable settings in the printer software. For example, choosing economy print resolution (about 180 dpi) will result in a faint print output. For high quality printing you need 720 dpi or above. The drawback of course is that the higher the dpi setting the slower the print speed. Also the printer will use a lot more ink.

Before printing you need to select the correct type of media for the particular application. When printing out photos for example, you need to use special photo quality glossy paper.

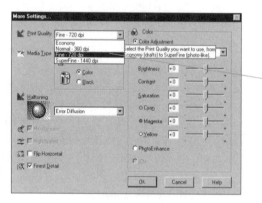

For quality printing you need a resolution of at least 720 dpi

Incorrect media selection can also cause problems. For example if you try to print out a colour photo on plain paper, the result will be less than impressive, as the coloured ink will bleed into the absorbent paper. You need to use special glossy paper for this purpose. Also, it's no good choosing the right kind of paper and then hoping the printer will correctly guess what it is – it won't. You need to select it in the printer software.

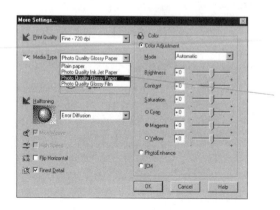

2 Tell the printer what type of paper you are using

Scanner Troubleshooter

Scanners are one of those so-so types of peripheral that are no means an essential part of a computer system but are nevertheless useful to have.

They are essentially quite simple machines with relatively little to go wrong inside them – most problems are presented by the software configuration.

However, while they may be simple machines, they can take a lot of setting up in order to get the best out of them and much of the associated terminology can be double Dutch to most people.

Covers

Scanner Doesn't Work | 116

Performance Issues | 117

Chapter Fourteen

Scanner Doesn't Work

Scanner Initialisation

One of the most common problems is to switch on the scanner and then see an error message stating that the scanner could not be found.

There are three main types of scanner – Sheet Fed, Hand Held and Flat Bed. This last is the one which will be familiar to most PC owners.

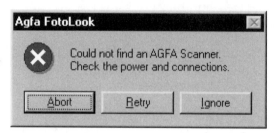

The reason for this is that many setups require the scanner to be switched on *before* the computer is powered up. This action is necessary to initialise the scanner's internal settings. If you want to turn your scanner on after your system is already up and running, go to the *Control Panel* and click the *System* icon. Select the *Device Manager* tab and then click the *Refresh* button. This sometimes fixes the problem. If it doesn't, turn your system off and reboot with the scanner turned on.

Incorrect resolution settings are one of the most common mistakes that people make when using scanners and invariably result in much larger image files than is necessary. This results in slow scans and image files taking a long time to open.

Transport Lock

If you've just installed a new scanner and it refuses to scan, check that the 'transport lock' isn't on. Many scanners are supplied with the scan head locked in position to prevent it sliding about during transportation. There is usually a slide switch of some sort with a lock/unlock symbol at the rear of the machine. Make sure this is in the 'unlocked' position.

Resource Conflicts

The next thing to check is that the scanner isn't in a resource conflict with another hardware device. Find out by going to the *Device Manager* in the *Control Panel*. See page 92.

Performance Issues

Scans are Very Slow

Firstly, it must be said that there are scanners and then there are scanners. Some operate much quicker than others so establish that yours isn't one of the slowcoaches before ripping it apart or taking it back to the shop.

Don't be taken in by the scanner manufacturers. At the moment claims of being able to scan at resolutions of up to 9600 dpi are the norm. These aren't real resolutions but rather 'interpolated' resolutions. A scanner able to scan at 600 dpi is the maximum you are ever likely to need.

Assuming an abnormally slow scan though, the usual reason is that the image is being scanned in at too high a resolution. This means the scan heads are having to read an incredible amount of data which will of course slow the scan speed down. In the scanner software, lower the scan resolution. Three hundred dpi is more than enough for most applications. In many cases even that is overkill. If you're scanning a photo for a web page for example, 75 dpi is ample.

A Scanned Image File Takes Ages to Open

The most likely reason is that the image is too big, i.e. it has been scanned in at too high a resolution. It's beyond the scope of this book to get into detail on this subject but suffice to say that in the vast majority of cases it is absolutely unnecessary to use a resolution above 300 dpi. The result will be literally indistinguishable from that at a higher resolution, while the image file size will be tiny in comparison.

Scanners place a heavy load on a computer's resources due to the large size of image files. For this reason they won't work very well on a low specified system.

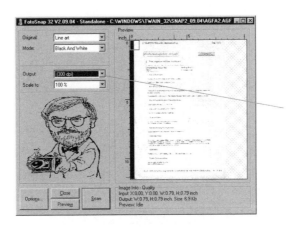

Select an image resolution of 300 dpi. This will be quite adequate for most purposes

To illustrate this point, a page of text scanned in at 300 dpi results in an image file of approximately 900 KB while the same page scanned at 600 dpi gives an image file of some 3.50 MB. This is nearly four times as big. In terms of clarity, the two images will be virtually indistinguishable.

When working with image files such as those produced by a scanner, always make sure you have no other programs running. Otherwise you run the risk of your system not having enough memory available to cope with the required task.

Another cause can be a system low in RAM. If, for whatever reason, you must scan at the highest possible resolution, you may find that you have to upgrade your system in terms of RAM capacity.

Having other applications running at the same time as the scan is in process reduces the amount of memory available to the scanner, thus potentially slowing things down.

Streaked or Smudged Images

It is essential to ensure that the glass scanning surface inside the scanner is spotlessly clean. Any dirty marks on it will be scanned in as part of the image. Clean the glass with a soft cloth prior to making the scan.

Grainy Images

Don't forget to keep the glass scanning surface spotlessly clean. Any marks on it will be scanned in as part of the scanned image.

This is caused by the colour depth of your display being set to 256 colours or less. Right-click on the *desktop*, select *Properties* and then *Settings*. Under *Colors*, choose 16 bits or higher.

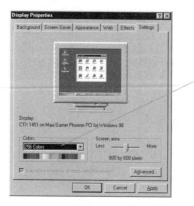

A colour depth of 256 or less will result in a grainy image. Set to 16 bits or above

Exported Image Looks Different to the Scanned Image

Sometimes when a scanned image is exported to an imaging program to be tweaked or whatever, it doesn't look quite the same – it might be a lot darker for example. This problem relates to the *Gamma* settings which are usually different from program to program. This can be corrected by using the imaging program's *Gamma* setting control.

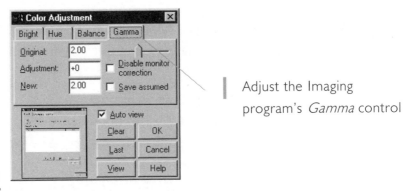

Adjust the Imaging program's *Gamma* control

Be careful when using the cropping tool in Preview mode. It is quite easy to crop out part of the image you want.

Part Of Scanned Image Missing

Most scanner software includes a *Preview* mode, which allows you to select or crop the part of the image you want to scan in. If, after the scan has completed, you find that part of your image is missing it will be because you have cropped it out.

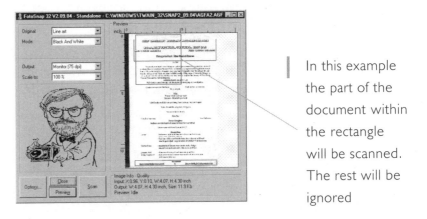

In this example the part of the document within the rectangle will be scanned. The rest will be ignored

Herringbone Patterns on Scanned Image

In some scans you may notice lettering or whatever, 'bleeding' through from the other side of the page. The way to avoid this is to use a sheet of black paper as a backing. Place this paper directly behind the page you are scanning, and the problem should be eliminated.

This is a well documented problem and is known as Moiré. We won't go into the technical details but basically Moiré manifests itself as a herringbone-like pattern of interference when a scan is made of a newspaper or magazine photo. To get rid of it you must use the Moiré control (sometimes called *Descreening*) in the scanner software. You can also try scanning at different resolutions to minimise the effect.

Garbled or Missing Characters in Text

When a scanned text document is imported into a word processor it needs first to go through a process known as Optical Character Recognition (OCR). This converts the image file into a text file that the wordprocessor can recognise. OCR programs are supplied with all scanners.

Unfortunately OCR software doesn't always produce perfect results – it makes the occasional mistake. While modern OCR software can be 99% accurate, this will still result in several errors on any one page of text.

One of the most common uses of a scanner is to scan text documents into a word processor. For this to work you will need an OCR program. Remember that these applications aren't perfect and will make mistakes.

This is the first thing to be aware of – it isn't a fault as such but rather the result of a technology that hasn't been perfected as yet.

The performance of any OCR package basically comes down to the clarity of the text being scanned in. The more clearly defined it is, i.e. dark characters on a white background, the better the result will be.

Similarly, small characters will be more difficult for the OCR program to read accurately. Also, the characters must be uniform – handwritten text will produce nothing but gibberish.

Modem Troubleshooter

A modem is a device that converts the digital data produced by your computer into the analogue data required for transmission along a telephone wire.

As these devices are required for Internet access, they are often considered as part and parcel of the Internet, which in some respects they are. For example, many of the problems usually associated with the Net, such as dropped connections, slow download speeds, etc., can also be caused by a faulty or incorrectly set up modem. Issues of this type are covered in the **Internet Troubleshooter**.

This chapter concentrates solely on what to do when your modem refuses to dial out.

Covers

Modem Doesn't Dial | 122

Modem Diagnostics Test | 123

Software Configuration | 124

Modem Driver | 126

Modem Passes Diagnostics Test | 127

Chapter Fifteen

Modem Doesn't Dial

Regardless of whether your modem is operational or not, there are two things which must be in place before you can connect to the Net and start pestering your pals with silly emails.

The first is a working telephone connection. This is straightforward enough to establish. Remove the modem cable from the phone socket and plug in a telephone. If you hear a dial tone, then it's working.

A common problem when trying to make a connection is to receive an error message which states that: *The Modem Is Busy or Not Responding.* The usual cause of this is that the modem is still running, i.e. it wasn't disconnected when you finished using it the last time. All you have to do is switch it off for a few moments before switching it back on again.

The second thing is, do you *have* a modem? There may be one plugged in to the computer, it may even work, but does the computer *know* it's there? Find out as follows:

Go to *Control Panel, System,* and *Device Manager.* Look for a category titled *Modem.* If it's there, then the system has found a modem. To find out if it's the *right* modem, click the + sign next to it. In the sub-category you should see the name and model of your modem. If it's the wrong one, then you'll have to remove it and then install the correct one. See page 126.

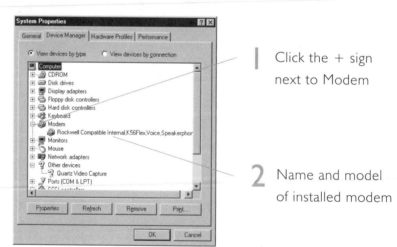

1 Click the + sign next to Modem

2 Name and model of installed modem

If there is no modem category at all, then the driver hasn't been installed. Go to the *Add New Hardware* wizard in the *Control Panel* and follow the instructions.

Modem Diagnostics Test

Having established that the modem is correctly installed, the next thing is to find out if it's working.

Do this by going to *Control Panel, Modems*. Click the *Diagnostics* tab and click the COM Port being used by the modem. Then click *More Info*. If, after a few moments, you see several lines prefaced with 'AT', then the modem is working and the problem is thus software related.

If you are running Windows ME then you have access to another modem diagnostics utility. This is called Network Diagnostics. This tool runs a check on your modem and terminal adapters and gives a status check plus a list of all the settings currently assigned to the devices. Go to Start, Programs, Accessories, System Tools. Click on System Information and then open the Tools menu.

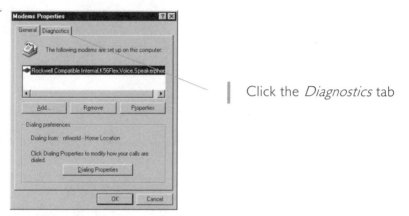

Click the *Diagnostics* tab

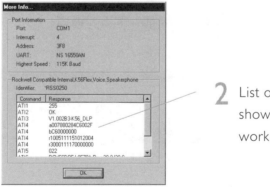

2 List of 'AT' commands show the modem is working OK

If you see nothing or a *Port Already In Use* message then the modem has failed the diagnostics test. This means that either the modem is faulty or your software is incorrectly configured. You could also have a corrupted modem driver. Check the software setup first.

Software Configuration

Firstly, ensure your modem is enabled by right-clicking it in *Device Manager* and then selecting *Properties*. Verify that the *Disable in this hardware profile* check box is cleared.

| Make sure this box isn't ticked

2 Click *Connection*

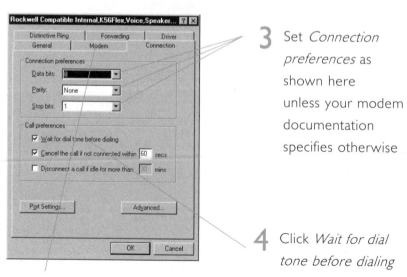

When checking your modem's settings, be sure to refer to the modem's documentation. If you don't have any documentation then use the settings shown opposite.

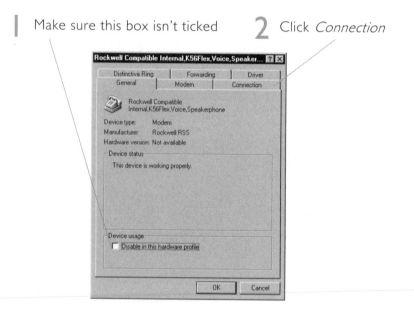

3 Set *Connection preferences* as shown here unless your modem documentation specifies otherwise

4 Click *Wait for dial tone before dialing*

5 Click the *Modem* tab

6 See what COM Port your modem is set to. Then check your modem documentation to see which port it *should* be set to. If necessary change it. NOTE: modems are usually configured to work off COM Ports 1 or 2

 If for whatever reason you do not want to listen to the sound of the modem making its connection every time you log on, you can switch it off by dragging the slider to the Off position in the Modem dialog.

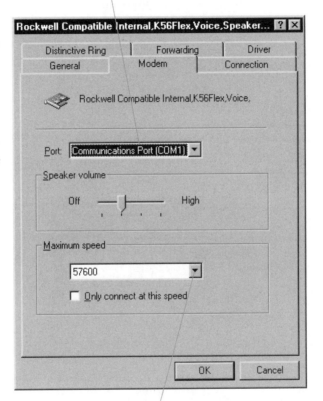

7 Select your modem's maximum speed here

If your modem's settings are as detailed in this section, then it is configured correctly. The next thing to check is the modem driver.

Modem Driver

Check the driver as follows:

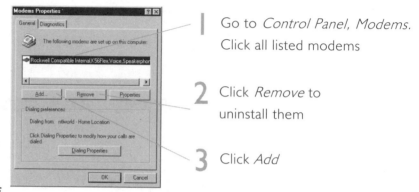

One of the most common reasons for a modem refusing to dial is a wrong or corrupted driver. Windows supplies a *Standard* driver which works with all modems and can be used to check for driver problems or even as a temporary driver.

1 Go to *Control Panel, Modems*. Click all listed modems

2 Click *Remove* to uninstall them

3 Click *Add*

4 In the next dialog box tick the *Don't detect my modem, I will select it from a list* box. Then click *Next*

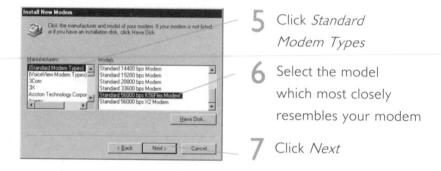

5 Click *Standard Modem Types*

6 Select the model which most closely resembles your modem

7 Click *Next*

What we are doing here is replacing the modem's driver with one supplied by Windows. This is a 'no frills' generic driver that will work with any modem.

When Windows has installed the driver, reboot the PC. On restart, run the diagnostics check again. If it responds successfully this time then the problem was being caused by the modem driver. Remove the Windows driver as described above, reboot again and Windows should now find the modem and prompt for the driver installation disk.

If none of the above steps solves the problem then you almost certainly have a faulty modem.

Modem Passes Diagnostics Test

 Analogue telephone lines were never designed with Internet access in mind. They are in fact totally unsuitable for this type of use as the bandwidth, i.e. capacity they offer, simply isn't enough to adequately cope with the volume of traffic the Internet generates. The strength of connection they offer is also very weak and is easily broken.

If you require a connection that is fast and reliable, seriously consider switching to ISDN or ADSL if it is available in your area.

This is a rare situation whereby you know the modem is OK (proved by the diagnostics test) and correctly configured, but it still won't dial out. There are two options left.

Firstly, make sure you have no other communications programs running and if you do, close them. Two of these programs running simultaneously could result in neither of them working.

Secondly, the communication program that your modem is using might be corrupt. Establish if this is the case by trying to make a connection with a different program.

Windows comes with several communications programs, any of which can be used for this purpose. *HyperTerminal* is as good as any.

1 Go to *Start, Programs, Accessories, Communications* and *HyperTerminal*

2 Type in a name. Any name will do

3 Click OK

...cont'd

4 In the next dialog box enter any valid telephone number in the *Area code* and *Phone number* boxes

Internet connection problems can also be caused by the communications program you are using. If you're sure your modem is working, configured correctly and that your phone line is OK then try using a different communications program such as *HyperTerminal* or *Phone Dialer.*

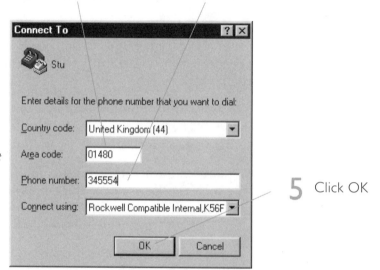

5 Click OK

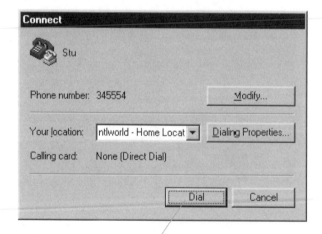

6 Hit the *Dial* button. If the modem now finally decides to dial then you know that your setup is OK. The problem lies in the original communications program that you were using. Re-install this program and everything should now be fine

Keyboard Troubleshooter

Some people might be surprised to see such a simple device afforded a section of its own, as they might also be with the **Mouse Troubleshooter** in the next chapter.

Nevertheless, it's a legitimate item of hardware which can cause problems just as any other.

It could be argued that as they are such an inexpensive item, why bother to repair them. However there are those who can get quite attached to a particular keyboard – it might suit their particular typing characteristics for example.

Whatever, this chapter details the problems you can expect to get and what you can do about them.

Covers

Keyboard Failure | 130

Cleaning Your Keyboard | 131

Keyboard Printing Strange Characters | 132

Caps Lock | 134

Chapter Sixteen

Keyboard Failure

The keyboard appears to be playing up. Problems can range from *Boot time error messages* to failure to get any characters to register on the monitor screen.

Connections

Do be sure that you haven't plugged your keyboard into the socket allocated to the mouse. In many PCs these are right next to each other.

The first thing to check is the connections, because in most cases this is the cause of the problem. Remaking them or jiggling the plug in the socket will often effect a cure.

Also, be aware that the keyboard socket is often right next to the mouse socket at the rear of the PC case and that each device will plug into the other's socket. It is an easy mistake to make.

Stuck Keys

Make sure you do not try to boot the PC with a key pressed down on the keyboard. This will often cause the keyboard to register an error when the PC is started up. This can happen with keyboards which are fouled up inside with muck and grime. It may not always be obviously apparent that a key is stuck down either, so check them all.

Given the low cost of a replacement keyboard it's a moot point as to whether they are worth the bother of taking apart to clean. Certainly if you are using one of the more sophisticated and thus expensive models, the answer is yes but otherwise probably not.

Keyboard Driver

Simple device though it may be, your system won't recognise and respond to the keyboard unless its driver is correctly installed. Check this out in *Device Manager* by going to *Control Panel, System, Device Manager.*

Keyboard Controller

This is a chip located inside the keyboard which interprets the keyboard commands and sends appropriate signals to the CPU. It's extremely rare for anything to go wrong with the keyboard controller but when it does, the keyboard will be useless. Throw it away and buy a new one. If the chip does fail, you will see an error message on the screen, usually in the bootup procedure.

Cleaning Your Keyboard

Spilling your mug of tea into the keyboard is obviously not recommended practice and the keyboard will not respond well to it.

However, it's not usually as catastrophic as you might think. All you have to do is shake out as much of the tea as you can. Then put the keyboard somewhere warm and wait for it to dry out. It should then be as good as new.

The major cause of keyboard problems is simply an accumulation of dirt and grime over a period of time. This can result in the mechanical switches under certain keys failing to make proper contact.

However, while this might work for some liquids, many others (soft drinks, etc.) also contain surprisingly large amounts of solids such as sugar, dyes and minerals. Even after the water has gone, there will be deposits left behind which can coat the switch contacts preventing proper operation. Sticky substances such as sugar can also cause keys to stick and increase the problem by attracting even more muck. Deposits such as these are best removed with distilled water or a mild form of spirit.

To remove stuff such as cigarette ash and crumbs, turn it upside down and gently shake or tap the back. If this doesn't dislodge the debris, you may have to remove a few keys. Before you do this though, make sure you note each one's place on the keyboard so you'll be able to put them back correctly. If possible, avoid removing the spacebar. A wire running through this key holds it level, and it can be difficult to remove and get back on correctly.

A very useful item for your troubleshooting toolkit is a tin of compressed air available at any good computer store. Apart from cleaning your keyboard, you can also use it to remove layers of dust from your circuit boards.

Once you've removed the keys, use a soft bristled brush to dislodge the material and then blow or brush it away. Replace the keys, plug the keyboard back into the computer and reboot.

If you are having trouble with specific keys, use switch contact cleaner on the offending key switches. With the keys removed squirt a little cleaner down into the contact. If there is a small plastic or rubber boot on the contact, you can usually lift it up a bit so you can reach the contact to spray it. Depress the key several times to work the cleaner in.

Keyboard Printing Strange Characters

There is a Windows setting which if set incorrectly can cause a problem which baffles many people.

The *Language* dialog shows the keyboard languages and layouts you have available and lets you easily add or switch between them.

A common problem is to inadvertently have your keyboard set to English (American). This will result in certain keys returning their American equivalents.

If your keyboard starts spitting out strange letters or accents or consistently prints a character to the screen that is different to the one you typed, it could mean the settings in this dialog are incorrect. For example you might be typing out a document one day and hit the £ symbol only to see a $ sign appear. This can be extremely perplexing as well as annoying if you do not know what is causing it.

1 Go to *Control Panel, Keyboards*

2 Click the *Language* tab

By using the Speed tab in the Keyboards utility, you can alter the speed at which the keys respond to your commands. This won't be of any noticeable benefit to the average user but to those who can type at great speed, it could be useful.

In the example given on the previous page, you will almost certainly discover that your keyboard is set to English (American). All you have to do is select English (British). Do this by clicking *Add* and from the drop down list select the language you want.

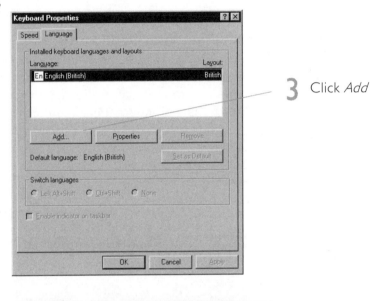

3 Click *Add*

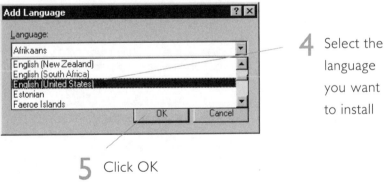

4 Select the language you want to install

5 Click OK

Your keyboard should now behave itself.

Caps Lock

An area in which the *Caps Lock* key can cause problems is when entering passwords. This is because passwords are case sensitive and the *Caps Lock* key setting determines whether you are typing in upper or lower case. If you inadvertently activate it, which is easily done, you will be typing your password in upper case. If the password was written in lower case, which it probably was, it simply won't work.

Never forget that passwords are case sensitive. This means that if a password was written in lower case it must be entered in lower case. If it isn't it won't work. If you find you are entering a password correctly without success, check that the Caps Lock key hasn't been pressed.

Adjusting Your Keyboard

If you so desire you can alter the way your keyboard responds, by means of the *Keyboard* dialog in the *Accessibility Options* utility. To access it, open the *Start* menu, select *Settings*, select *Control Panel*, and click *Accessibility Options*. From here, you can set up additional keyboard features that: let you use the *Shift, Ctrl,* or *Alt* keys by pressing one key at a time; ignore brief or repeat keystrokes; and let you hear warning tones when you press the *Caps Lock, Num Lock,* or *Scroll Lock* keys.

A good way of preventing the Caps Lock key being inadvertently activated is by configuring the PC to produce a tone when the key is pressed. This is done in the Keyboard dialog in the Accessibility Options utility, which you can find in the Control Panel.

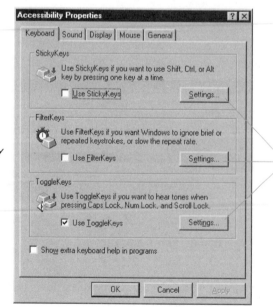

Adjust your keyboard settings here

Mouse Troubleshooter

The humble but nevertheless essential mouse is the simplest device on a computer system, with little to go wrong inside. For this reason mice are very cheap and easy to replace.

As with their real life namesakes, they are very busy little creatures and similarly prone to dirt. This tendency is what gives rise to most problems with these devices.

Covers

Mouse is Dead | 136

Mouse Movement is Jerky | 137

Turbo Charge Your Mouse | 138

Mouse Keys | 140

Chapter Seventeen

Mouse is Dead

Firstly, make sure that the mouse is connected to the correct port at the rear of the PC's case and that the connection is good. Then check to see that the mouse has been seen by Windows in *Control Panel, System, Device Manager*. If it has, it will be listed here. If not then the mouse driver isn't installed correctly.

Mice may be very simple and basic devices but like any piece of hardware they need a driver to 'introduce' them to the system. If you're having mouse problems make sure the driver is present and correct.

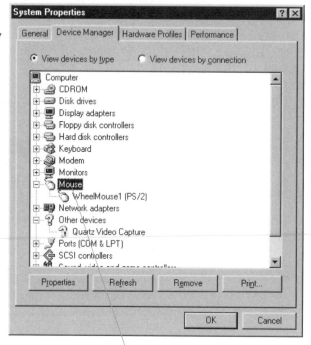

Mouse driver is installed

If the mouse has been correctly installed, then make sure that it is not conflicting with another device. See **Resource Conflict Troubleshooter**.

Mouse Movement is Jerky

If you find you are constantly having to clean your mouse to keep it functioning smoothly, you could consider buying one of the new breed of super mice. These devices are solid state, i.e. have no moving parts, thus will never require cleaning. They do however cost considerably more.

The mouse's motion is not smooth and fluid. When you move it, the cursor moves in an erratic or jerky fashion. There are two main causes of this type of behaviour:

Dirt

Like keyboards, mice are devices that are handled a great deal and therefore get dirty very quickly. They are particularly receptive to dirt thanks to the rubber ball which rolls about on the desktop picking up muck as it does so.

Up end the mouse and remove the rubber ball – give it a good clean. Then have a look inside the mouse itself where you will see some little plastic rollers (usually three). In the middle of each, you will probably see a line of dirt running right round the circumference. This is the cause of the problem. The dirt is preventing the ball from making a smooth contact with the rollers resulting in jerky movement of the cursor. Clean the dirt off and the mouse will be as good as new.

If your mouse's buttons aren't functioning properly, the inner workings of the mouse could be causing the problem. Take the mouse apart and spray contact cleaner onto the contacts and switches inside the mouse, depressing the buttons several times to work the cleaner in.

Mouse Pads

The performance of a mouse depends to a great extent on the surface on which it is being used. Avoid smooth shiny surfaces such as a polished table or desktop.

The surface on which you run the mouse can greatly affect its performance. They don't work well on smooth, shiny surfaces, an element of 'grip' is needed. Too much grip though will hinder movement. Experiment with different materials until you find one that suits. If you are using a mouse pad, make sure it's clean and flat. Also remember the old adage – you get what you pay for. This applies equally to mouse pads. Some are definitely better than others.

Turbo Charge Your Mouse

Even if your mouse is working fine, you can improve its performance by changing settings in *Mouse Properties*. Go to *Control Panel* and then click the *Mouse* icon. This dialog box lets you tinker with many aspects of your mouse settings.

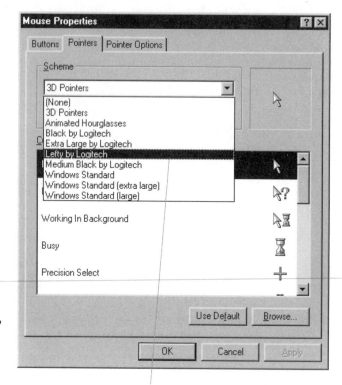

If for any reason you have lost the mouse pointer on the screen, you can configure Windows to show the position of the pointer when you press the Ctrl key. You can set this up by going to Control Panel, Mouse, Pointer Options.

The *Pointers* dialog allows you to change the on-screen pointer to something you like better or more suitable to the work in hand. Windows also provides a number of pre-configured schemes

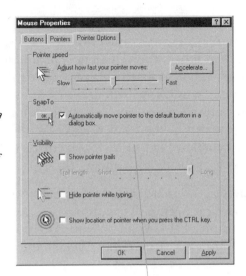

 Most mice are supplied with a right hand configuration, which is fine if this is the hand you use. If, however, it isn't, you can change the mouse to a left hand configuration in the Buttons dialog box.

2 The *Pointer Options* dialog allows you to change how your pointer appears and moves on the screen. You can set the pointer speed and the amount of acceleration it has, as well as whether pointer trails appear after it when it moves and how long such trails will be. You can also set your pointer to automatically jump to the highlighted button of each new dialog box

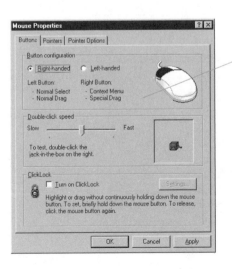

3 The *Buttons* dialog allows you to change what each mouse button does. You can also configure the mouse for left or right hand use here

Mouse Keys

It's not unknown for a mouse to suddenly stop working for some reason – its connection to the PC may have been knocked loose, there may be a problem with the mouse's driver or the mouse itself may have failed. When this happens you'll find you are unable to control your computer. This can be serious if you are in the middle of a project and haven't saved it yet. Without the mouse how will you be able to get to the *Save* button? You stand a real chance of losing all your work.

One way to guard against this possibility is to activate the *MouseKeys* option. This allows you to control the cursor with the numerical keypad on your keyboard. To do this go to *Control Panel, Accessibility Options* and click the *Mouse* tab.

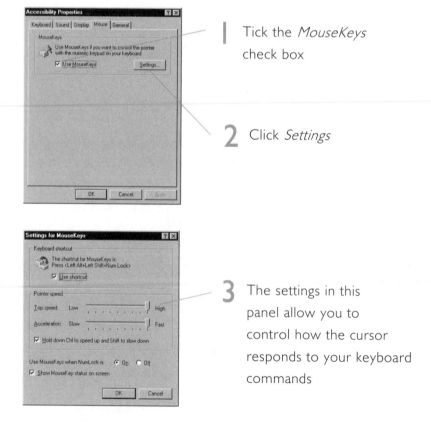

1 Tick the *MouseKeys* check box

2 Click *Settings*

3 The settings in this panel allow you to control how the cursor responds to your keyboard commands

Network Troubleshooter

A computer network is a group of individual computers all physically linked to each other and able to share the available resources.

For a network to function, all the individual computers must be compatible and speaking the same language, i.e. a common protocol. As with most other computer faults, problems usually arise as a result of incorrectly configured software.

Covers

Isolating the Problem | 142

One or More PCs Malfunctioning | 143

Network Adapters | 144

Network Client | 145

Network Protocols | 146

Computer Names | 148

File and Print Sharing | 149

Troubleshooting Network Hardware | 150

Unable to Share Resources | 152

Pinging | 153

Chapter Eighteen

Isolating the Problem

A bridge is a device that connects two or more networks using the same protocols.

A gateway is the same as a bridge except it allows the various networks to communicate via differing protocols.

A router is an intelligent gateway as it directs data along the most efficient route.

A hub is a device used in a STAR network to link the various computers.

Troubleshooting networks can be quite a challenge as the nature of the setup introduces many more variables, i.e. instead of just one computer, there will be several plus all the cabling and other hardware.

To have any realistic chance of successful faultfinding, you must at the very least, have a basic understanding of networks – the various layouts and relevant hardware, etc.

One of the first things you have to do is establish exactly what type of network you're dealing with. You need to know how many computers are in the network, where they are and details of any associated hardware such as routers, bridges, gateways, etc.

For example, the most basic type of network is called a local area network (LAN), and might be a simple setup consisting of two or three PCs in the same office and linked together with a bit of coaxial cable. Alternatively, several hundred machines might be hooked up within the confines of a large building such as a stock exchange via a series of routers and heavy duty network cable.

Once you have some idea of what you're up against, you can start narrowing things down using a process of elimination. Find out which PCs are affected. Are there problems with one PC, several PCs, or every computer on the network?

Remember that there are basically four things that can go wrong with a network:

- One or more PCs malfunctioning

- A problem with the server

- A problem with a hub, router, bridge or gateway

- A problem with the cabling or its connections

Once you have established in which of these areas the problem lies, you are well on your way.

One or More PCs Malfunctioning

The usual problem is one of the PCs not being able to communicate with one or more of the other PCs on the network.

Most network problems are caused by incorrectly configured software. Things to check are:
- *Network clients*
- *Network protocols*
- *Computer names*
- *File and Print Sharing*
- *Network adapters*

Firstly, establish where the problem lies. If the suspect PC can 'see' just one of the other computers, this proves the PC itself is OK and that the fault is somewhere in the network. See the **Troubleshooting Network Hardware** section.

If, on the other hand, the PC is totally isolated from all the other computers, then the problem lies with the PC itself or a segment of the network common to it. Which is it though – the PC or the network?

There are any number of things that can go wrong with the PC itself so the quickest of the two possibilities to rule out is the network. This is very easily checked by doing what is known as a 'ping' test (see end of this chapter for details). This procedure basically involves sending a small packet of data to a specific computer, which then sends it back to the computer which sent it.

What we have to do is to ping another computer on the network (PC 'B') from the suspect computer (PC 'A'). If the ping test is successful, it proves that the network hardware between the two computers is sound. The problem therefore must lie with PC 'A'. However the ping test might fail. In this case we still don't know if the problem lies with PC 'A' or with the network.

So we do another ping test – this time from PC 'B' to PC 'A'. If the test fails again then the network between the two computers must be faulty. See the **Troubleshooting Network Hardware** section. If, however, it is successful this time, then we know that the network is OK. This means that the suspect PC (PC 'A') is faulty and must be investigated.

In the case of a faulty PC the problem is almost always to do with the software setup. The first thing to check is your network adapter.

Network Adapters

There are two main methods of connecting a PC to a network. One is by means of a network adapter card, which is physically installed in the same way as a modem or sound card. The second is to use *Dial-Up Networking (DUN)* in the form of the *Dial-Up Adapter* which is supplied by Windows. This method utilises your modem for the network connection. NOTE: if you are using *DUN* you will need to make sure your modem is working.

Most network cards are supplied with an inbuilt diagnostic utility which determines whether or not the card is working.

Whichever method you use, it first needs to be correctly installed. Check by going to *Control Panel, Network, Configuration*.

If you are using DUN for your network connection, the modem takes the place of a network card adapter. This introduces yet another factor to be considered in the event of a failed network connection.

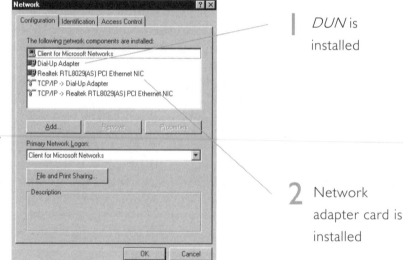

1 *DUN* is installed

2 Network adapter card is installed

If your chosen method of connection is not installed then you must install it with the *Add New Hardware* wizard in the *Control Panel*. In the case of a network adapter card you will need its driver installation disk. *DUN* will require the Windows CD.

Once you have ruled out the network adapter as a cause of the problem, check the *network client*.

Network Client

A *network client* is the part of the network software which allows you to access data stored on disks on the other computers on the network. The most commonly used client is *Client for Microsoft Networks.* Make sure it is installed as follows:

A network client enables your computer to connect to other computers on the network and make use of the available network resources.

| Go to *Control Panel, Network*

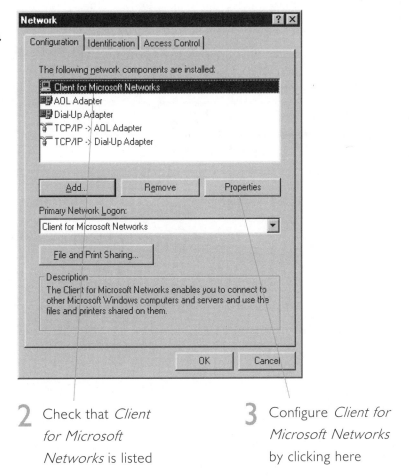

2 Check that *Client for Microsoft Networks* is listed

3 Configure *Client for Microsoft Networks* by clicking here

The next possibility is the *network protocol.*

Network Protocols

A network protocol is basically a 'language' that allows networked computers to communicate with each other. For this to work all the computers must have the same protocol installed and selected.

For a network to function, all the PCs in that network must be speaking the same lingo (protocol). If they aren't then they won't be able to understand each other. There are many different protocols but the most commonly used in networking is TCP/IP. If you are experiencing any problems with your network ensure all the computers are using the same protocol.

There are several different protocols used in networking which include *NetBEUI, IPX/SPX* and *TCP/IP*. Of these, *TCP/IP* is by far the most popular and is automatically installed when *Client for Microsoft Networks* is installed. Check by going to *Control Panel, Network*.

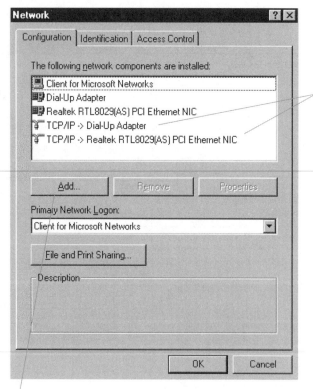

Installed protocols

2 If the required protocol is not installed then you will need to install it. Click *Add*

The more protocols you have installed on your system, the greater the likelihood of connection problems as the various protocols can interfere with each other. Delete any protocol which isn't being used.

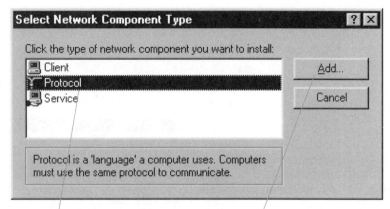

3 Click *Protocol*

4 Click *Add*

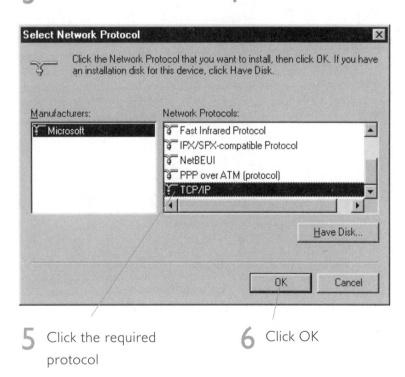

5 Click the required protocol

6 Click OK

Having established that your protocols are in order, it's time to make sure that your *computer names* are correct.

Computer Names

Before a computer will be recognised by a network it must first have a name which is unique to that network. It must also have a *Workgroup* name that is identical to the *Workgroup* names of all the other computers on the network. Check this out as follows:

Try to use names which are descriptive and convey useful information. This makes it easier for everyone using the network to find the resources they need.

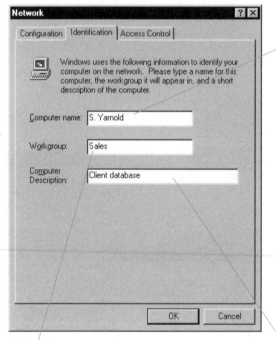

The name entered in this box must be unique. No other PC on the network can have this name

2 The name in the *Workgroup* box must be exactly the same for all the computers on the network

3 In this box you can enter a descriptive name. For example it could indicate the type of information available on the PC

The last item of software setup to investigate is *File and Print Sharing*.

File and Print Sharing

The whole purpose of networked computers is to facilitate the sharing of the information and resources on those computers. Before this can happen however, *File and Print Sharing* must be activated. If it isn't the computers will not be able to 'see' each other.

File and Print Sharing is what allows other computers on the network to access the resources available on your computer.

Go to *Control Panel, Network*

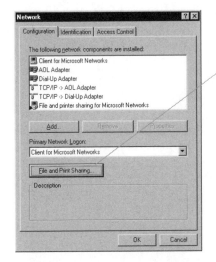

2 Click *File and Print Sharing*

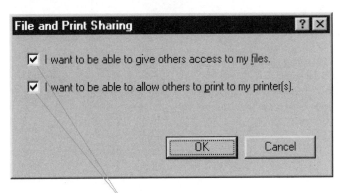

3 Tick these boxes to enable *File and Print Sharing*

The PC is now correctly configured and set up.

Troubleshooting Network Hardware

Having established that the problem is in the network, the next thing is to narrow down which section of the network is faulty. The thing to remember is that the fault is going to be common to all the affected computers and to determine where this is, you will need to know the layout of the network.

The way a network is laid out is known as its topology and depends to a large degree on the number of computers to be connected and their location. The two main types are called BUS and STAR and which one is used depends mainly on the size of the proposed network.

When troubleshooting a network it pays to know as much about that network as possible. Things to establish include the number of computers, their location, the network's topology and what hardware it is using.

If the size of the network is not likely to be too great, then a BUS topology will be used. Here the computers will be connected to each other along a single line of network cable, the individual stations being known as *Nodes*. This arrangement is shown below.

If however you need a large network or can envisage a potential need for one, then a STAR topology will be the best choice. With this system, all the computers are given their own cables which are then all connected up to each other via a central unit called a hub. See opposite page.

A network's layout is known as its topology. Two of the most common topologies used are BUS and STAR.

BUS Network

STAR Network

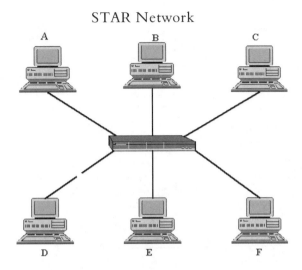

When investigating a network don't forget about hardware such as bridges, routers etc. Problems with these devices often result in a major failure of a network as they are common to so many, if not all, of the computers.

While the BUS method has the advantage of being the cheaper, as it needs less cable and does not require associated hardware, it does suffer from a fundamental flaw. Should there, for any reason, be a break in the network, then the PCs on either side of the break will become isolated from each other.

This is demonstrated in the diagram opposite. Here we can see that PCs 'A', 'B' and 'D' can communicate with each other but not with PCs 'C', 'E' and 'F' due to a break in the network. PCs 'C', 'E' and 'F' can communicate with each other but not with PCs 'A', 'B' or 'D'. Given these symptoms, it doesn't take a genius to work out which section of the network is broken.

When troubleshooting networks try and think logically. By establishing which parts of the network are working and which aren't, it's often possible to locate the problem without too much effort.

However, with the STAR system, as shown above, all the PCs are individually connected to a central hub. It's clear from this that any break in the network can only affect one of the PCs (PC 'D' in the diagram). However, if several or all of the PCs were out of action then the problem would have to lie with the hub as this would be the only component common to all the affected PCs.

From the above it should be clear that a logical analysis of the situation will reveal the approximate, if not exact, location of the break in the network.

Unable to Share Resources

The first thing to check is that *File and Print Sharing* is installed as already described in this chapter. Make sure that this is done on all the PCs that will be sharing these *resources*.

Next, check that you have *Resource Sharing* set up correctly.

The *File and Print Sharing* facility allows other network stations to access resources on your computer in the same way as *network client* allows you to access resources on their computers.

1 Right-click the *resource* (file, printer etc.) you wish to share with the network

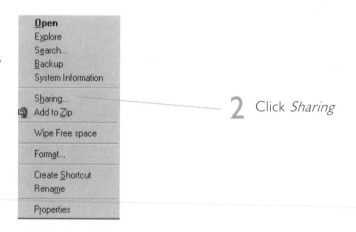

2 Click *Sharing*

If you right-click on a *resource* you want to share and don't see 'Sharing' on the menu, you will find that you don't have *File and Print Sharing* installed. See page 149.

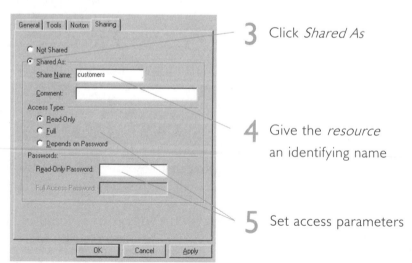

3 Click *Shared As*

4 Give the *resource* an identifying name

5 Set access parameters

Pinging

Pinging is a procedure used for locating breaks in networks. Basically it involves sending a packet of data to a specific computer which will then send the data back to the original computer. A successful ping proves that the section of the network pinged is intact.

Before you can do a ping test though, you'll first need to find out the current Internet IP address for the computer you want to ping to.

Do this as follows: On the target computer go to *Start, Run*, and type in WINIPCFG. This will load the Windows IP Configuration Utility, which will show you the IP address that is currently assigned to that computer.

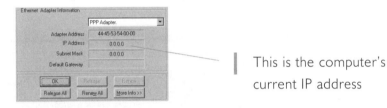

This is the computer's current IP address

Now go back to the computer you are pinging from and access the DOS prompt by clicking *Start, Programs, Accessories*. (In Windows 98, *Start, Programs*.) Open a DOS window and at the prompt type PING followed by the IP address of the target PC. Hit *Enter* and if the test is successful you should see almost immediately several lines beginning with *Reply from xxxxxx*, where *xxxxxx* is the IP address you entered.

2 Type PING followed by the IP address of the computer being pinged

However if the test fails you will see several lines saying *Request Timed Out*.

It's also possible to check an individual computer by getting it to ping itself.

The procedure for doing this is as follows:

A more advanced form of ping is called Tracert. A trace route will show you all of the routers, hubs, and systems in your network. Not only this, it will also tell you the time taken between hops, as well as the number of hops. This info can help you determine where network bottlenecks are occurring and give you feedback on the overall health of the connection. The procedure is exactly the same as for a ping test except instead of typing PING at the DOS prompt you type TRACERT.

At the DOS prompt type PING LOCALHOST and then hit *Enter*. LOCALHOST is a reserved host name that maps to a reserved IP address (127.0.0.1) that represents your computer. When you type PING LOCALHOST, the messages are local to your computer; no packets are sent to the network

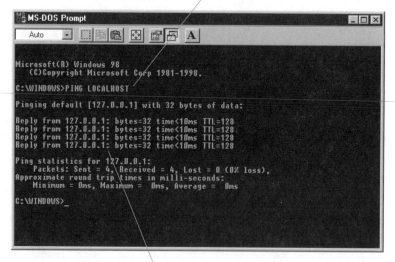

2 If pinging LOCALHOST is successful, you will receive four replies from IP address 127.0.0.1, as shown above. If the ping command is unsuccessful, you will receive a message that says LOCALHOST is unknown

Internet Troubleshooter

An Internet problem can be strictly defined as a problem caused by one of the routers and links that make up the interconnected set of networks that comprise what we know as the Internet. But a more general definition is probably more practical – if your connection to a site via the Internet isn't working or working poorly, you have an Internet problem.

These can be caused by anything from software configuration problems on your PC to system failures at the site you are connecting to.

Covers

Unable to Connect to the Internet | 156

Intermittent Connections | 158

Slow Connections | 160

Unable to Access Particular Sites | 162

Common Error Messages | 163

Chapter Nineteen

Unable to Connect to the Internet

The first thing to check is that your modem is functioning as it should. See **Modem Troubleshooter**.

Next, you need to verify your Internet software setup.

If you are successfully connected you will see two little monitors on the right hand side of the taskbar. If the monitors are 'off' no data is being transferred. If the monitors are 'on' data is being transferred.

1   Go to *Control Panel, Dial-Up Networking*. Under the *General* tab make sure your ISP's phone number is entered correctly

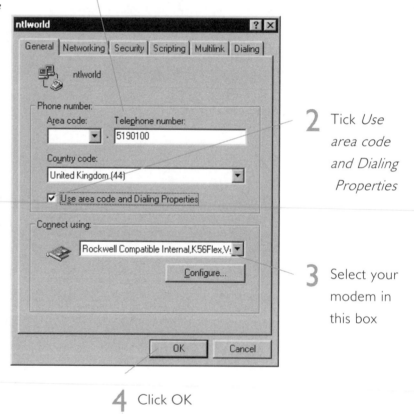

2   Tick *Use area code and Dialing Properties*

3   Select your modem in this box

4   Click OK

This procedure assumes a connection has already been set up. The dialog is also available from *My Computer*, and also by selecting *Start, Programs, Accessories, Communications, Dial-Up Networking*.

Make sure you are entering the correct user ID and password when prompted.

Never assume that your ISP is totally reliable. Many of them aren't, especially the ones providing a cheap or free service. Remember, you always get what you pay for.

5 Type in your *User name* and *Password* in these boxes. Make sure you enter the password in the right case

External Problems

Consider the possibility that your ISP might be down – it does happen, particularly if you are using one of the new breed of ISP who offer a free service. Remember that any service or product that is free is not usually of the highest quality. Give them a ring and check.

Intermittent Connections

You lose your connection at periodic intervals for no apparent reason. There are several causes of this problem.

Idle Disconnect

If your connection keeps breaking after exactly the same period, then do the following:

Go to *Dial-Up Networking* (see page 156). Click your Internet connection then click *Properties, Dialing*

A dodgy Internet connection might actually have nothing to do with your setup but rather the ISP's. If the connection is consistently poor simply sign up with a different ISP. Alternatively you could have two separate accounts. If you're having a problem with one then you can switch to the other and vice versa. This is a perfectly feasible proposition with the plethora of ISPs currently offering a free service.

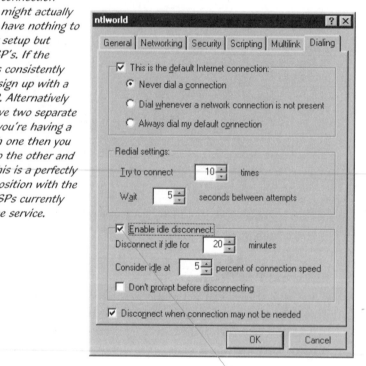

2 Remove the check mark from *Enable idle disconnect.* This is a safety feature which automatically disconnects you after a set period of Internet inactivity. This prevents you from clocking up a huge phone bill if for some reason you don't manually log off

Call Waiting

If this feature is activated, it can break your Internet connection when another call comes in.

Try disabling it as follows:

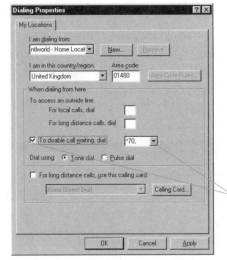

1 Click *Modems* in *Control Panel*

2 Click *Dialing Properties*

3 Tick *To disable call waiting, dial* and in the drop down box select *70

Viruses and screensavers are a possible cause of iffy connections. Never discount the possibility of a virus. Run a virus checker. As for screensavers, well, unless you bought your monitor from Noah, you really shouldn't be using them as these days they are completely unnecessary and in fact cause more problems than you would have without them. Get rid of them.

Programs/Devices Which Activate Suddenly

Applications such as *Advanced Power Management* and screensavers can break your connection when they 'kick in'. Try disabling them.

Remove any other devices connected to the line which might be causing interference such as phones, answering machines and fax machines. All of these can result in a lost connection.

Slow Connections

If you are using the Internet in the evenings and at the weekend, don't expect super fast performance. These are the times when most other people will also be online, inevitably slowing it down.

The most common cause of this is an overloaded site or network. The more people using the Net at any one time, the slower it will respond, as all the systems resources are shared. The same applies to individual sites and ISPs. If this is the cause of the problem you will notice it occurs mostly in the evenings and at weekends when everyone else is also online. Either put up with it or try again later.

One way to speed up a slow connection is to disable loading of graphics and sound in your browser. Do this by going to *Control Panel, Internet Options*. Click the *Advanced* tab. Under *Multimedia*, clear one or more of the *Show pictures, Play animations, Play videos* and *Play sounds* check boxes.

Disabling some of the media options in your browser, such as sound and graphics, can boost the browser's performance considerably.

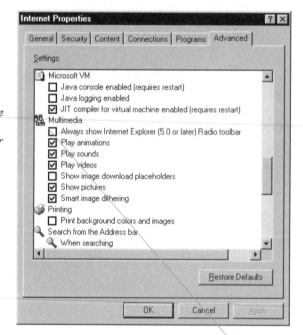

Unchecking some of the multimedia options such as sound, video and pictures will speed up your browser

Modem Speed

Have you got your modem revved up?

| Go to *Control Panel, Modems, Properties*

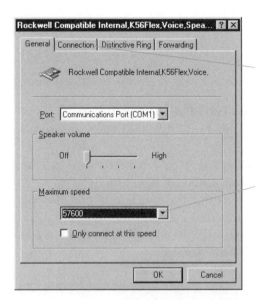

3 Click the *Connection* tab and then the *Port Settings* button

2 Select your modem's maximum speed here

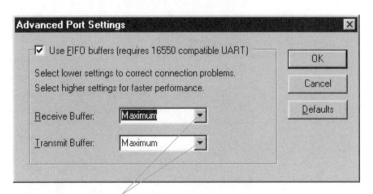

4 Set the *Transmit & Receive Port Buffers* to *Maximum*

Unable to Access Particular Sites

Probably the most common reason for being unable to access a particular site is simply typing in the wrong address. If this is the case you will get a The page cannot be displayed error message. The address must be entered exactly as it reads.

There are many reasons why you may be unable to access a particular site and usually you will see an error message of some sort to explain why. The following are just some of the possible reasons:

- Site temporarily down

- Site closed down

- Access denied for some reason

- A broken or out-of-date hyperlink

Content Ratings Advisor

It's also possible that someone has been fiddling about with the *Content Ratings Advisor*. This utility purports to allow a degree of censorship on what type of web site can be accessed by users of the PC. It does work to a certain extent but unfortunately can also block access to sites with absolutely no offensive content. To check out this possibility have a look in *Control Panel, Internet Options, Content, Enable.*

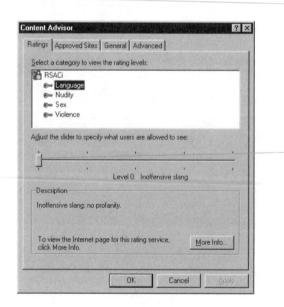

Dragging the slider to the right decreases the level of protection

Common Error Messages

Bad Request – The address you typed is incorrect. The URL may not exist or you may not have authority to access the document on the server.

Unauthorised – You're treading on restricted ground. The page you've tried to access is only available to people authorised by the host or those with the correct password. Sites can also restrict access to those people who are connecting from a particular domain: for instance, you might only be able to access a site if you connect via a .edu or .gov domain or via a particular country domain.

Some sites can only be accessed via a particular domain. In other words they are not open to the general public. This is often the case with educational and government sites.

Forbidden – The page you're trying to view is password protected or restricted in some other way.

Not Found – The particular page you're looking for can't be found on the server. It may be that the page no longer exists or that it's been moved to another location or renamed.

Internal Error – There's something wrong at the web site itself. As their server is not functioning correctly, it's unable to provide you with the requested web page.

Service Unavailable – This is a 'temporarily out of order' sign and it means either the server that hosts the site is currently not working or is unavailable, your ISP's server is down, or your own system is not working.

Connection Refused by Host – Like the *Forbidden* and *Unauthorised* messages, this one usually means you've tried to access a password protected site or one that's restricted to users from particular domains.

It's very easy to lose your Internet connection without realising it. If you find you are suddenly unable to access any site at all, check this possibility first.

Host Unavailable – The site's server is currently down.

Host Unknown – It could be that the site's server is down (as with the previous message) or that your modem lost the connection.

It's not unknown for some sites to become literally overwhelmed by the volume of traffic they are experiencing. In these circumstances the server hosting the site will refuse to allow any more 'hits'. All you can do is try again later when things may have quietened down.

Network Connection was Refused by the Server – This usually means you've come across an overworked server that can't handle any more users.

Permission Denied – This is an FTP message which you'll see if you try to upload a file to an FTP site and the site administrator doesn't want you to. You may also see it if you try to download a file using the wrong syntax or simply when the site is too busy to handle an upload.

Unable to Locate the Server – The particular server where the site is located cannot be found – either it no longer exists or you've got the URL (address) wrong.

Email Troubleshooter

Problems with sending and receiving email are invariably the result of incorrectly configured ISP and email software.

Once you know how to correctly set up these programs however, your emailing woes will be over.

Covers

Internet Connection | 166

ISP Software Setup | 167

Email Software Setup | 169

Message Rules | 171

Problems Sending Email | 172

Chapter Twenty

Internet Connection

Before you can send and receive email, three things need to be in place.

- An Internet connection

- Correctly configured ISP software

- Correctly configured email program

If you are unable to connect to the Internet, you will get nowhere fast. Emails don't just magically appear on your PC, they need a source and a physical route to your computer. The system works as follows:

The sender of the email types out the message in his or her email program, logs on to the Net and then hits the send button. The email program establishes contact with the sender's ISP's computer and then sends the email to a program known as an *SMTP (Simple Mail Transfer Protocol) server.*

The SMTP server now contacts another software program, known as a *domain name server* and requests the best available route. After checking, the domain name server will pass on the requested information.

The SMTP now sends the message to *your* SMTP server, from where it is transferred to another server called a *POP (Post Office Protocol) server.* Here the message will be held.

When you next log on to the Internet you will be informed that you have mail waiting. The POP server retrieves the message and sends it to your email program.

Before you can receive your email though you must be logged on to the Net and this requires a modem connection.

If you are experiencing any problems making a connection, go to the **Modem Troubleshooter**.

ISP Software Setup

Having established that your computer is actually connected to the Internet, you now need to check your ISP software setup. Do this as follows:

Many people are confused by the issue of POP and SMTP server settings.

Basically, POP and SMTP are an Internet language used for the transmission (SMTP) and reception (POP) of email messages. It is essential that they are correctly entered in your software and will be supplied by your ISP. A typical example of a POP setting would be 'POP.ntlworld.com' where 'ntlworld.com' is your ISP.

1 Go to *Control Panel* and click *Dial-Up Networking*

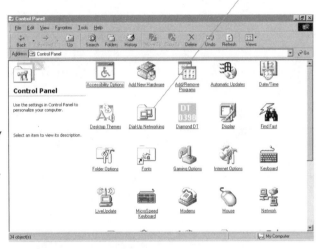

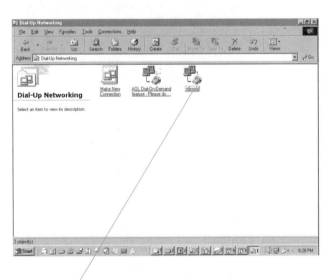

2 Right-click your ISP's icon and then click *Properties*

TCP/IP is an Internet protocol which allows your computer to communicate with your ISP's computer.

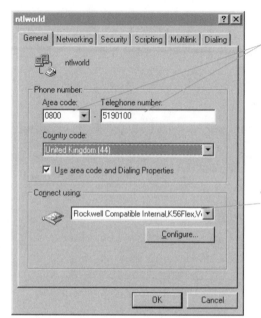

3 Under the *General* tab, make sure you have correctly entered the area code and the ISP's telephone number

4 Your modem must be selected in this box. If not, click the *Configure* button to set it up

5 Click the *Networking* tab

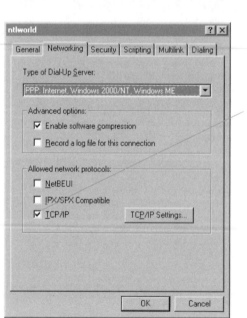

6 Ensure the TCP/IP network protocol has been selected. This is the protocol used for Internet connections

Your ISP software is now correctly set up.

Email Software Setup

Having established that your ISP software setup is correct, you must now do the same with your email program.

Open the program (Outlook Express, Eudora, etc.) by clicking on it and go to the *Tools* menu. Click *Accounts* and then click *Mail*.

Follow the steps as described below.

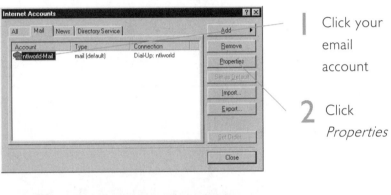

1 Click your email account

2 Click *Properties*

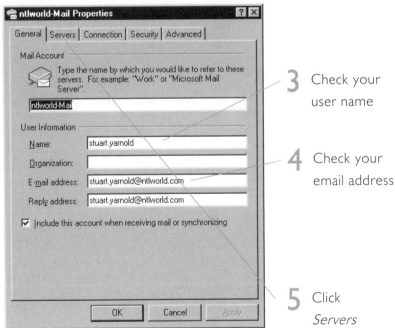

3 Check your user name

4 Check your email address

5 Click *Servers*

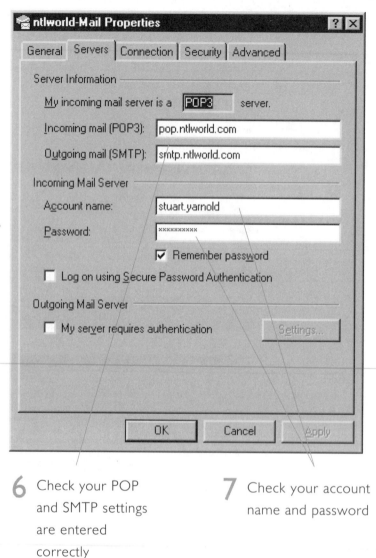

POP and SMTP stand for Post Office Protocol and Simple Mail Transfer Protocol respectively. This is basically an Internet language that allows the transmission and reception of email.

6 Check your POP and SMTP settings are entered correctly

7 Check your account name and password

Your email program is now correctly configured.

Message Rules

A setting in your email software that can interfere with received messages is *Message Rules*. This is a feature of email programs which allows you to block emails from a specified address or with certain content. It's also possible to block all emails. Make sure there isn't an incorrect setting here. Find out as follows:

The Message Rules utility is a useful email feature. For example you can use it to stop emails from specific addresses. Blocking unwanted Spam is a typical application. You can also use it to block emails over a certain size.

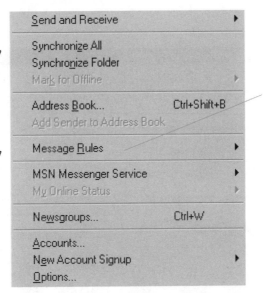

1 Select *Tools, Message Rules*. In the sub-menu click *Mail*

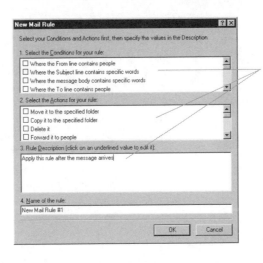

2 These settings allow you to specify, to a certain degree, the permissible content of received emails

Problems Sending Email

Problems here are usually caused by the same things that affect email reception, i.e. software setup. The most likely of these will be an incorrect SMTP server setting in your email setup. Check this by doing the following:

Should you ever wish to send sensitive information by email and are worried that it might fall into the wrong hands, consider using an email encryption program. This will make it unintelligible to anyone but the recipient, assuming he or she has the same program with which to decipher it.

If you are in any doubt as to what your server settings should be, then just contact your ISP.

1 Open your email program and click *Tools, Accounts, Mail*. Then click *Properties* and click the *Servers* tab

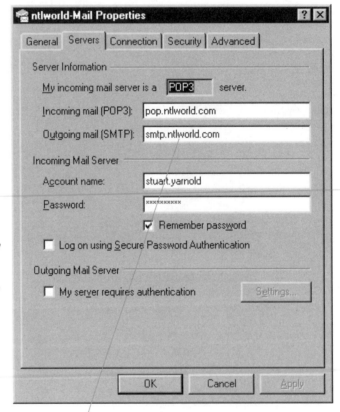

2 Enter your SMTP server setting here. This will usually be 'SMTP' followed by the name of your ISP as shown above

Check that all other settings are correct as described in the **ISP Software Setup** and **Email Software Setup** sections of this chapter.

Troubleshooting Utilities

Any PC user will be familiar with a common Windows utility called *ScanDisk* for the simple reason that it runs automatically when Windows is incorrectly shut down.

However this is just one of many troubleshooting aids that Windows supplies and there are probably very few people who are aware of all of them and how to access them and put them to good use.

The purpose of this chapter is to familiarise the reader with the more useful of these applications.

Covers

ScanDisk | 174

Disk Cleanup | 175

Disk Defragmenter | 176

System Restore (Windows ME) | 177

Maintenance Wizard | 178

System Information | 179

Dr Watson | 180

System Configuration Utility | 181

System File Checker (Windows 98) | 182

Startup Disk | 183

How to use a Startup Disk | 184

Third Party Utilities | 185

Chapter Twenty-one

ScanDisk

ScanDisk is a Windows utility that is provided for the purpose of checking your drives for problems and errors. It does a physical check of the disk's surface and also an analysis of the way data is stored on it. If it finds any problems it can usually repair them. Potential problems include incorrectly addressed data clusters which means the system might not be able to recover the data when asked to do so. Another more serious problem is that of physical damage to the magnetic surface of the disk. When *ScanDisk* comes across a damaged sector, it simply marks it as 'Bad'. Any files you save subsequently will be kept away from this sector.

If you don't want ScanDisk to run automatically after an incorrect shutdown you can disable it by going to Start, Run and typing MSCONFIG in the box. Under the General tab click Advanced then tick the Disable ScanDisk After Bad Shutdown box.

You will find that *ScanDisk* presents you with the option of two tests – *Standard* and *Thorough*. *Standard* will check all files and folders for errors while *Thorough* will check files and folders plus the surface integrity of the disk. Then you can choose whether to let *ScanDisk* automatically repair any errors it finds or simply advise you of what it's found.

You will at some stage notice that when Windows is shut down incorrectly, the next time it boots, *ScanDisk* will run automatically, although you can disable this if you wish. This is Windows playing safe as most drive errors are caused by incorrect shutting down.

It really isn't necessary to go out and buy an expensive utility program to troubleshoot and maintain your PC. Windows comes with all the utilities you need for this purpose.

As a final note, when running *ScanDisk*'s *Thorough* test, make sure you have something else to do as it can take simply ages depending on the speed of your PC and size of the drive. Also make sure you have no other applications running, including screensavers, as these can interfere with the utility.

You can access *ScanDisk* by going to *Start, Programs, Accessories, System Tools*. Alternatively go to *Start, Run* and type SCANDISK in the box before hitting *Enter*.

Disk Cleanup

Temporary file folders, particularly the Temporary Internet Files folder, can fill up at an alarming rate especially if you browse the Net regularly. It's all rubbish, none of it is needed, so clear them out occasionally. You will find them in the Windows folder on your hard drive. Disk Cleanup provides an easy way to do this.

Over a period of time, a PC's hard drive will become cluttered up with data which is no longer needed. This has the inevitable result of decreasing the amount of space available for what *is* needed. This isn't so much of a problem today with the enormous capacity of the hard drives currently available, but only a few years ago, most definitely was. To this end disk cleanup utilities were devised.

Microsoft's version, *Disk Cleanup*, offers the option to delete files from your *Browser* cache, *Recycle Bin* and *Temp* directories, as well as the uninstall files for Windows itself. Access *Disk Cleanup* by going to *Start, Programs, Accessories* and *System Tools*. Click on the *View Files* button for a preview of the files marked for deletion. The *More Options* tab lets you remove other optional Windows components and uninstall programs.

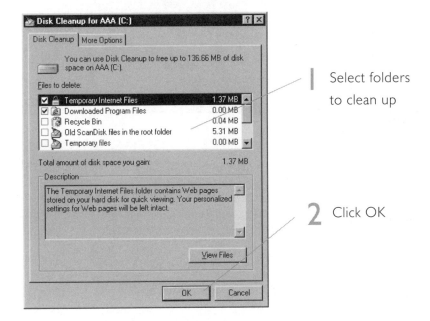

Select folders to clean up

2 Click OK

Disk Defragmenter

Defragging a hard drive can take a very long time, a factor dependent on the speed of your PC and the size of the drive being defragmented.

Fragmentation is the process whereby fragments of files become scattered randomly throughout a drive's disk or disks over a period of time. This has the effect of slowing down the performance of the drive as it is constantly having to hunt about to find the various parts of a file in order to reconstruct it.

Defragmenting is a physical reversal of this process and is carried out with the *Disk Defragmenter* utility. Any type of magnetic drive – hard drive, floppy disk or Zip disk – can be defragged with *Disk Defragmenter*. Access *Disk Defragmenter* by going to *Start, Programs, Accessories, System Tools*.

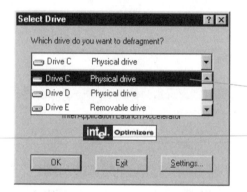

Select drive to be defragmented

Before you defragment a drive, make sure there are no applications running in the background which can suddenly activate. Typical examples are screensavers and Advanced Power Management. These types of application can stop the defragging process.

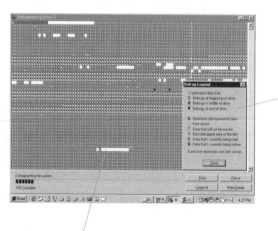

2 Legend indicating what type of data the disk clusters hold

3 Defragmentation in progress

System Restore (Windows ME)

The big drawback with *System Restore* is that if you roll back to a point before a particular program was installed, that program will not work after restoration. If you want to use the program again, you must re-install it.

If changes to hardware, software, or settings on your computer have left it in a dodgy condition, you can use *System Restore* to undo the changes made to your computer and thus restore it to working order. This procedure is done without losing data and is completely reversible.

System Restore keeps track of changes at specific intervals, as well as when events such as program installations occur. You can also create your own restore points, to record settings as they were just before you make changes. This allows you to revert to a more stable state or period, by choosing a restore point on a date prior to when a change occurred.

For example, if you accidentally delete program files or program files become corrupted, you can restore your computer to how it was before those changes occurred.

While *System Restore* will 'send your PC back in time' as it were, it won't cause you to lose recent data such as your email messages and Favorites.

System Restore will not cause you to lose your personal files. Items like documents, email messages, and browsing history are saved when you revert back with *System Restore*.

You can access *System Restore* by going to *Start, Programs, Accessories, System Tools*. If it doesn't open then go to *Control Panel, System, Performance, File System, Troubleshooting* and make sure the *Disable System Restore* check box is cleared.

System Restore is a new Windows utility available only to users of Windows ME.

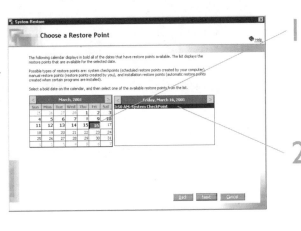

1 Choose the date you want to go back to. Available dates are highlighted

2 Select a system check point

Maintenance Wizard

This isn't really a troubleshooting tool but is nevertheless useful in that it helps you to get the best performance from your system. You can use *Maintenance Wizard* to make your programs run faster, check your hard disk for problems, and free up hard disk space. By scheduling these utilities to run on a regular basis, you can make sure that your computer is always performing at its best.

You can access *Maintenance Wizard* by going to *Start*, *Programs*, *Accessories*, *System Tools*.

The *Maintenance Wizard* is designed for those who forget or are too lazy to maintain their system. This allows you to automate the process to run at a time when you are not using the PC.

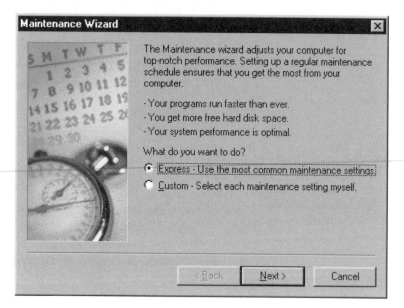

The program gives you the option to use *Express* (most common settings) or your own *Custom* settings.

If you choose *Custom* settings, you'll have the option of scheduling each task separately. You also have the option to set parameters for each task.

Tasks you can automate with *Maintenance Wizard* include *ScanDisk*, *Disk Defragmenter* and *Disk Cleanup*.

Make use of this useful application as it will help optimise the performance of your system.

System Information

Again, not strictly speaking a troubleshooting utility but the information it can give you about your system can be extremely useful, not just in the event of a problem, but at any time. You can access *System Information* by going to *Start, Programs, Accessories, System Tools*.

The *System Summary* will give you precise details regarding your operating system, BIOS chip, CPU, motherboard, etc.

Hardware Resources is a mine of information regarding resource conflicts and IRQs.

Components lists all the hardware devices in your system and gives details of their status (OK or not OK), resources assigned to them and which driver they're using.

Amongst other things, *Software Environment* informs you about any programs currently running and which applications start automatically with Windows.

System Information also logs any software and hardware changes made to your computer. This is information that can be very useful when troubleshooting.

System Information also gives you access to even more troubleshooting and diagnostic utilities which can be found under the *Tools* menu.

Dr Watson

This is more of a diagnostic utility and when activated it takes a snapshot of your system, and displays any errors it finds. If you choose *View, Advanced View* from the menu, you can see some information on the state of your system.

Dr Watson will give you all kinds of useful information on topics such as *Diagnosis, System, Tasks, Startup, Kernel Drivers, User Drivers, MS-DOS Drivers* and *16-bit Modules.*

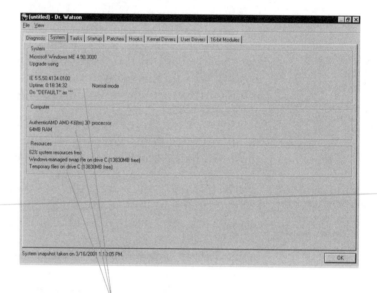

Dr Watson can give all sorts of useful information about your system

Dr Watson was designed as a faultfinding aid to service technicians, the idea being that when something goes wrong, the program will record exactly what happened.

To access *Dr Watson* go to *Start, Run* and type DRWATSON in the box. Then hit *Enter*. You will then see a new icon on the right hand side of your taskbar. Click this and the program will open.

System Configuration Utility

The *System Configuration Utility* automates the routine troubleshooting steps that Microsoft Technical Support engineers use when diagnosing issues with the Windows configuration. You can use this tool to modify the system configuration through a process of elimination with check boxes.

If you are using Windows 95, type SYSEDIT in the Run box. This will open the System Configuration Editor which is 95's version of the System Configuration Utility.

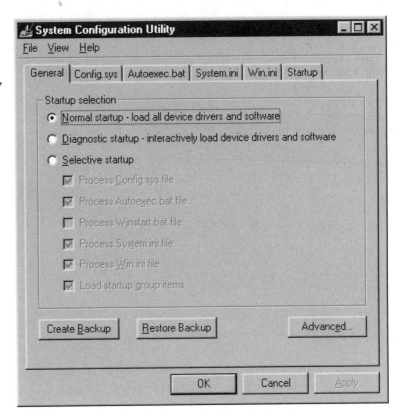

If you are running Windows 98 or ME, you can access this utility by going to *Start, Run* and then typing MSCONFIG in the box. Then hit *Enter*.

Windows 95 users need to go to *Start, Run* and type SYSEDIT in the box. This will open up the *System Configuration Editor* which is 95's version of the *System Configuration Utility.*

System File Checker (Windows 98)

This useful utility allows you to check the integrity of your Windows system files. To run the program click *Start, Run,* and type SFC in the box. Then click OK.

Users of Windows ME don't have access to SFC as the utility runs automatically behind the scenes without the user ever being aware of it.

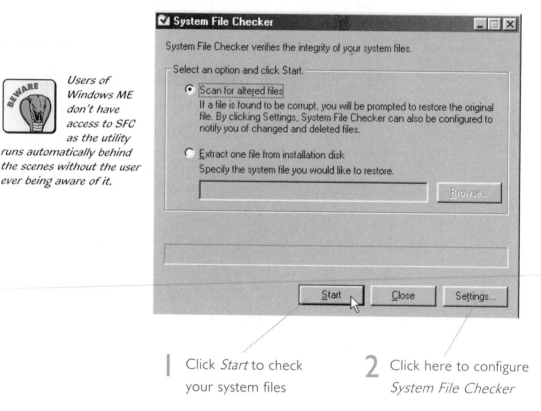

| Click *Start* to check your system files

2 Click here to configure *System File Checker*

If the utility finds any corrupted files it will either replace them automatically from a backup copy or advise you of the fact and ask what you want to do.

Alternatively you configure SFC to check certain types of files and ignore others.

This utility can also be used to extract individual files from the Windows CD.

Startup Disk

The Windows *Startup Disk*, sometimes called a boot disk, is the most important item in your troubleshooting toolkit. If you haven't done it yet, then make one now. When the inevitable happens one day and you can't get your PC to boot, this disk will give you a way back into your system. Without it you will be able to do nothing.

Disaster often strikes without any warning and this accurately describes a PC which refuses to boot up. This is when the Windows *Startup Disk* can come to your rescue. In the case of a PC which refuses to start or when Windows refuses to load normally, a *Startup Disk* lets you access your system via a command prompt (DOS mode).

This single floppy disk loads a command line version of Windows and includes repair and diagnostic tools to help get your machine on its feet again. Remember this though – when you need a *Startup Disk*, you can't make one. In order to be prepared when disaster strikes, you need a *Startup Disk* already made and to hand. Go to *Control Panel, Add/Remove Programs*.

You can only make a *Startup Disk* via Windows. However, it's precisely when you can't get into Windows, that you will need it. Make sure you have one safely tucked away somewhere.

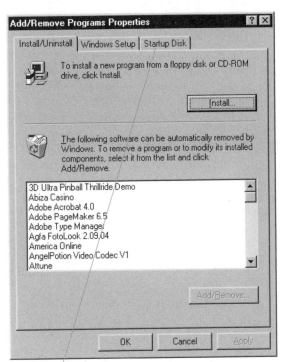

Click the *Startup Disk* tab and then follow the instructions

How to use a Startup Disk

Insert the *Startup Disk* in the floppy ('A') drive, and reboot the PC. You will see a *Startup Menu* with three choices. Choice one is *Start Computer With CD-ROM Support*. This is usually what you will want. Select it and hit *Enter*. You'll see some text go by as Windows sets up your CD-ROM drive and scans your peripheral cards. Then you will see a message that says *Preparing to start your computer. This may take a few minutes, please wait...*

Remember that using either Format or FDisk on your hard drive will erase all information on the drive. Use these utilities with great care.

When startup is complete, you will see an A:\> prompt. Be aware that the *Startup Disk* causes your CD-ROM drive to shift up by one letter, i.e. if it is normally drive 'D', it will now be drive 'E'. The extra drive letter is used for an in-memory disk drive created by the startup process. This is where the *Startup Disk* utilities are stored. The reason for this is that the utilities and startup routines won't all fit on a single floppy disk unless they are compressed. During the startup process, the utilities are decompressed and stored in the in-memory drive.

When using a Startup Disk, the computer's CD-ROM drive letter will be shifted up one. This is normal and is not a fault.

Let's take a look at a few of these utilities and see how you can use them to examine or repair your hard drive.

SCANDISK is a utility which checks your disk drives for errors, and can fix most hard drive problems. To check your drive using SCANDISK, type SCANDISK C: at the prompt.

EDIT is the MS-DOS text editor. You may need this to create or repair AUTOEXEC.BAT, CONFIG.SYS, or .INI files. Type EDIT

FORMAT formats hard and floppy drives. Type FORMAT C:

FDISK controls the partitioning of hard drives. Type FDISK C:

SYS is used to transfer the operating system to a disk drive and make it bootable. If you suspect the boot files on your hard drive are damaged, type SYS C: to restore them.

Third Party Utilities

There are several diagnostic and repair utilities available on the software market, which provide many of the functions described in this section. The most popular ones are *Norton Utilities, Nuts & Bolts* and *First Aid*.

As is usually the case with most things, there are pros and cons with these programs. On the plus side, many of the applications within these programs are actually better than the Windows versions and work much more quickly. On the down side it must be said that some of them can actually cause more problems than they solve. It must also be remembered that they can be a serious drain on the systems resources. Plus of course, you have to pay for them.

Remember that utility programs which run in the background monitoring what's happening in your PC, take up a great deal of your systems resources and can on occasion be the cause of problems themselves.

Probably the most popular utility on the market is *Norton Utilities* which is basically a collection of various tools. This program starts you off with a graphical interface called *Utilities Integrator*, which is the launching pad for all its tools. These can be classified into four groups – Diagnostic/Repair, Troubleshooting, Preventative Maintenance and Performance Enhancement.

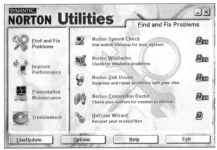

In the first group you will find tools such as *System Check*, which with one click will examine your entire PC for problems and repair any it finds. *Disk Doctor* performs a series of surface analysis checks on your drive's disks and automatically carries out repairs if necessary. (Windows' version of this tool is *ScanDisk*.) *Connection Doctor* will assist in any connection problems you might have, such as connecting to the Internet. It will also check all your communication ports and modem. *Unerase Wizard* is a particularly useful facility that can help you to recover files that have been lost or deleted.

Troubleshooting tools include:

Registry Editor which allows you to get behind the Windows interface and edit the Windows registry which contains all your systems settings. Messing with the registry can be a hazardous operation so Norton includes an *Undo* feature. *System Information* is another very useful facility and it does just what its name suggests. With this tool you can get information on just about anything in your system.

Preventative Maintenance tools include:

System Doctor which sits quietly in the background monitoring what's going on in your PC and will give you advance warning of impending problems such as your hard drive running low on space. *Wipeinfo* will remove any trace of selected files from your drives. *Protection* adds extra data recovery options to the recycle bin.

Performance Enhancement tools include:

Speed Disk which is a defragmentation utility that works considerably faster than the defrag tool supplied by Windows. *Space Wizard* provides a safe means of identifying, moving, compressing or deleting files in order to free up disk space.

From all this it can be seen that this utility, and others of its ilk, provide very useful applications which can be used to help keep your PC performing at its best. It must be remembered though that they are not fool proof and indeed some of the lower quality utilities not only miss many problems but often *cause* problems. They can also, particularly on slower PCs, be a serious drain on the systems resources, slowing the computer down even further.

Index

A

Accessibility Options   134
Add New Hardware
    wizard   58, 62, 84, 97, 122, 144
Add/Remove Programs   28
Advanced Power Management   17, 159
  Disabling   44
AUTOEXEC.BAT files   32, 41

B

Beep codes   17–18
  AMI   23
  Award   23
  Phoenix   24
BIOS   12, 18, 22, 52, 179
  Setup program   52
  Startup display   22
Blue Screen of Death   107
Boot floppy disk   36, 46
Boot procedure   21–22, 130
Boot Time Error Message   21
Bootup   16
Browser cache   175
BUS   150

C

Call Waiting   159
Caps Lock   134
CDs
  Auto play   66
  CDs don't play properly   64
  Cleaning   64
  Scratched   64
Client for Microsoft Networks   145
Close Program   101, 103
Close Program dialog box   101
Colour depth   78
COM Port   123
Compatibility Mode   57
CONFIG.SYS files   32, 41
Content Ratings Advisor   162
Control Panel   11, 20, 28, 62, 82, 104, 122, 138
CPU   19, 74, 107, 130, 179
Crashes   12, 70, 100, 102–103
Ctrl+Alt+Del   10, 12, 26, 71, 101, 103

D

Defragmenting   106
Descreening   120
Desktop colour depth   106
Device
  Manager   20, 30, 35, 58, 62, 91, 104, 107–108, 122
  Error codes   97
Device Status   92
Diagnostics   123
Dial-Up Adapter   144

Dial-Up Networking (DUN)   144
Direct Memory Access Channels (DMA)   90
Disable Fast Shutdown   38
Disk Cleanup   73, 175
Disk compression   68
Disk Defragmenter   46, 55, 176
Display   76
  Blank   80
  Colour depth   78
  Distorted   77
  Electrical interference   76
  Flickering   76
  Focus   80
  Moiré patterns   80
  Refresh rate   76
  Resolution   78
  Scrambled   77
  Shadowing/ghosting   80
  Wrong size display   80
DMAs   90
Domain name server   166
DOS   47
DOS prompt   28, 48
Dpi setting   114
Dr Watson   180
DVDs
  Auto play   66
  Cleaning   65
  DVDs won't play   65
  Scratched   65

Economy print resolution   114
Electrical interference   76
Electromagnetic interference   86
Email   166
Email software setup   169
Exit sound file   39
Expansion cards   54

Fan   105
Fatal Exception Errors   107
FDISK   59, 184
Floppy drive   63, 67
Format   36, 67, 184
Formatting   31, 48, 59
Fragmentation   176
Freeware   11
Freeze   10
Frozen PC   101

Gamma settings   119
General Protection Faults   106
Generic driver   126
Graphics card   17, 20
  Connections   20
  Driver   79
  Replacement   20
  Resource conflict   20

Hard disk controller   58
Hard drive   52
  Access   54
  BIOS setup program   52
    Password   52
  Error messages   60
  Failure   52
  Failure symptoms   53

Formatting   59
Partitioning   59
Performance issues   55
   Compatibility Mode   57
   Drive running slowly   55
   Viruses   56
Power supply   53
Resource conflicts   54
Thrashing   72
Hardware Resources   179
Heat   105
Hyperterminal   127

I/Os   90
Icons   103
IDE devices   22
IDE HDD Auto Detection   52
Idle Disconnect   158
Illegal Operations   108
Imaging   112
Ink cartridge   110
Input/Output Port Addresses (I/O)   90
Insufficient Memory Errors   108
Intermittent connections   158
Internet
  Error messages   163
  Slow connections   160
    Modem speed   161
  Software setup   156
Interrupt Request Channnels (IRQ)   90
Invalid Page Faults   107
IP address   153
IP Configuration Utility   153
IPX/SPX   146
IRQs   90
ISP   157
ISP software setup   167

Keyboard   16, 130
  Adjusting   134
  Cleaning   131
  Connections   130
  Controller   130
  Driver   130
  Lights   16
  Stuck keys   130

LEDs   16
Lens cleaning disk   64
Local area network   142
Lockups   10, 12, 70, 102–103

Maintenance Wizard   178
Manufacturers' beep codes
  AMI   23
  Award   23
  Phoenix   24
Memory   70
Message Rules   171
Microsoft product key   31
Modem   122
  Communications programs   127
  Driver   126
  Software configuration   124
Modem diagnostic test   123

Moiré   80, 120
    Reduction control   80
Monitor   17
    Splash screen   17
Motherboard   9, 17
Mouse   136
    Cleaning   137
    Pads   137
    Pointers   138
    Properties   138
MS-DOS prompt   153

NetBEUI   146
Network   142
    Adapters   144
    Client   145
    Computer names   148
    File and Print Sharing   149
    Hardware   142
        Bridges   142
        Gateways   142
        Hubs   142
        Routers   142
    Local area network   142
    Ping test   143
    Protocols   146
    Resources   152
    Topology   150
Nodes   150
Numerical keypad   140

Operating system   179
Optical Character Recognition (OCR)   120

Partitioning   59
Password   52, 134, 157
Peripherals   14, 54
Ping   143, 153
PING LOCALHOST   154
Plug & Play   22
POP server   166
Post Office Protocol   166
Power cable   16
Power off button   12
Power On Self Test (POST)   22
Power supply   16, 105
    Fan   16
Primary DOS Partition   59
Primary Master   52
Primary Slave   52
Print speed   114
Printer   110
    Cleanliness   113
    Connections   111
    Ink cartridge   110
    Nozzle cleaning utility   110, 113
    Pause printing   111
    Poor print quality   113
        Symptoms   113
    Software settings   114
    Test page   110
Printer cable interface   110
Printer software   114
Protected mode driver   58

RAM   70, 72, 74, 85, 90, 102, 106, 112, 118
RAM chips   70
    Replacing   70
Read/write heads   55

Recycle Bin   175
Refresh   116
Refresh rate   76
Registry   12, 28, 30, 107
Registry Editor   186
Reset button   12, 101
Resolution   78
Resource conflicts   35, 54, 62, 90, 104
  Identifying   92
  Resolving   93
  Symptoms   90
  Windows startup   35
Resource Sharing   152
Retained Memory   74
Run Time Error Message   21, 106

S

Safe Mode   27, 77, 100, 107–108
  Starting in   27
Safe Recovery   49
Scan resolution   117
ScanDisk   12, 29, 46, 53–54, 60, 101–
  102, 107, 174
Scanner   116
  Initialisation   116
  Performance issues   117
    Gamma settings   119
    Grainy images   118
    Moiré   120
    Streaked or smudged images   118
  Preview mode   119
  Resolution   117
  Slow scans   117
  Transport lock   116
SCANREG/RESTORE   30, 35, 107
Screensavers   105–106, 159, 174
  Disabling   105
Secondary Slave   52
SMTP server   166
Software   14
Sound   82
  Card installation   84
  Powered speakers   83

Problems
  Crackling or noisy   86
  Distorted   87
  Jerky/intermittent sound   85
  Volume control   83
Standard CMOS setup   52
Standby mode   17
STAR   150
Startup Disk   28, 36, 47, 54, 59, 183
  How to use   184
Startup folder   34, 46
Startup Menu   27, 32
Startup programs   34, 43
Step By Step Confirmation   32
Substitution   14
Surge suppressor   16, 76, 105
Swap file   72
System Configuration Editor   33, 181
System Configuration Utility   33, 181
System File Checker   182
System files   28, 30, 54
System Information   179
System instability   8, 100
  Causes   102
    Conflicts   104
    Damaged hard disk drives   102
    Heat   105
    Incorrect shutting down   102
    Power supplies   105
    RAM fragmentation   102
    Running too many applications   103
    Screensavers   105
    Startup programs   104
    Viruses   102
  Error messages   106
    Fatal Exception Errors   107
    General Protection Faults   106
    Illegal Operations   108
    Insufficient Memory Errors   108
    Invalid Page Faults   107
    Windows Protection Errors   108
  Symptoms   100
System performance   70
System resources   71, 85
System Restore   177
SYSTEM.INI files   32, 41

T

TCP/IP   146
Telephone connection   122
Temporary folders   40
   Temp folder   40
   Temporary Internet Files folder   40
Temporary Internet Files   40
Topology   150
Transport lock   116

Windows
   CD product number   31
   Clean installation   36, 46, 48, 107
   Initialisation files
      AUTOEXEC.BAT files   32, 41
      CONFIG.SYS files   32, 41
      SYSTEM.INI files   32, 41
      WIN.INI files   32, 41
   Protection Errors   108
   Setup   31, 46
      Error messages   49
      From DOS   47
   System files   182
   Upgrading   46
Workgroup   148
Write protection   68

U

Unshielded speakers   77
USB hubs   85
USB ports   85
USB speakers   85
User ID   157

V

Virtual Memory   71, 107
Viruses   11, 46, 56, 102, 108
Voltage spikes   105

W

WAV file   82
WIN.INI files   32, 41